DATE DUE			

FARMS and FARMERS in art

Fine Art Books for Young People

AMERICAN HISTORY *in Art*
The BIRD *in Art*
The BLACK MAN *in Art*
The CAT *in Art*
CIRCUSES *and* FAIRS *in Art*
The CITY *in Art*
DEMONS *and* BEASTS *in Art*
FARMS *and* FARMERS *in Art*
The HORSE *in Art*
KINGS *and* QUEENS *in Art*
MEDICINE *in Art*
MUSICAL INSTRUMENTS *in Art*
POLITICS *in Art*
The RED MAN *in Art*
The SELF-PORTRAIT *in Art*
The SHIP *and the* SEA *in Art*
SPORTS *and* GAMES *in Art*
The WARRIOR *in Art*
The WORKER *in Art*
The OLD TESTAMENT *in Art*
The NEW TESTAMENT *in Art*

FARMS and FARMERS in art

By Helen B. Harkonen, Designed by Robert Clark Nelson ■ Lerner Publications Company, Minneapolis, Minnesota

Prepared under the supervision of Sharon Lerner, Art Editor

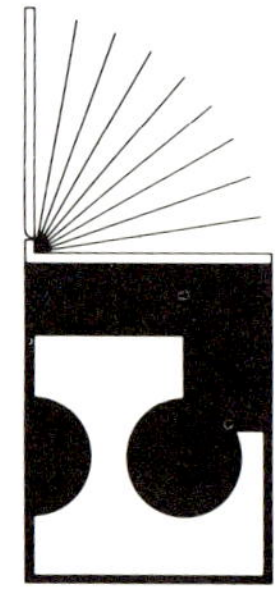

Fourth Printing 1971

 International Standard Book Number: 0-8225-0152-X. Library of Congress Catalog Card Number: 64-8204. Manufactured in the United States of America. Published simultaneously in Canada by J. M. Dent & Sons Ltd., Don Mills, Ontario.

Corn Husking, (1860); by Eastman Johnson, Everson Museum of Art, Syracuse.

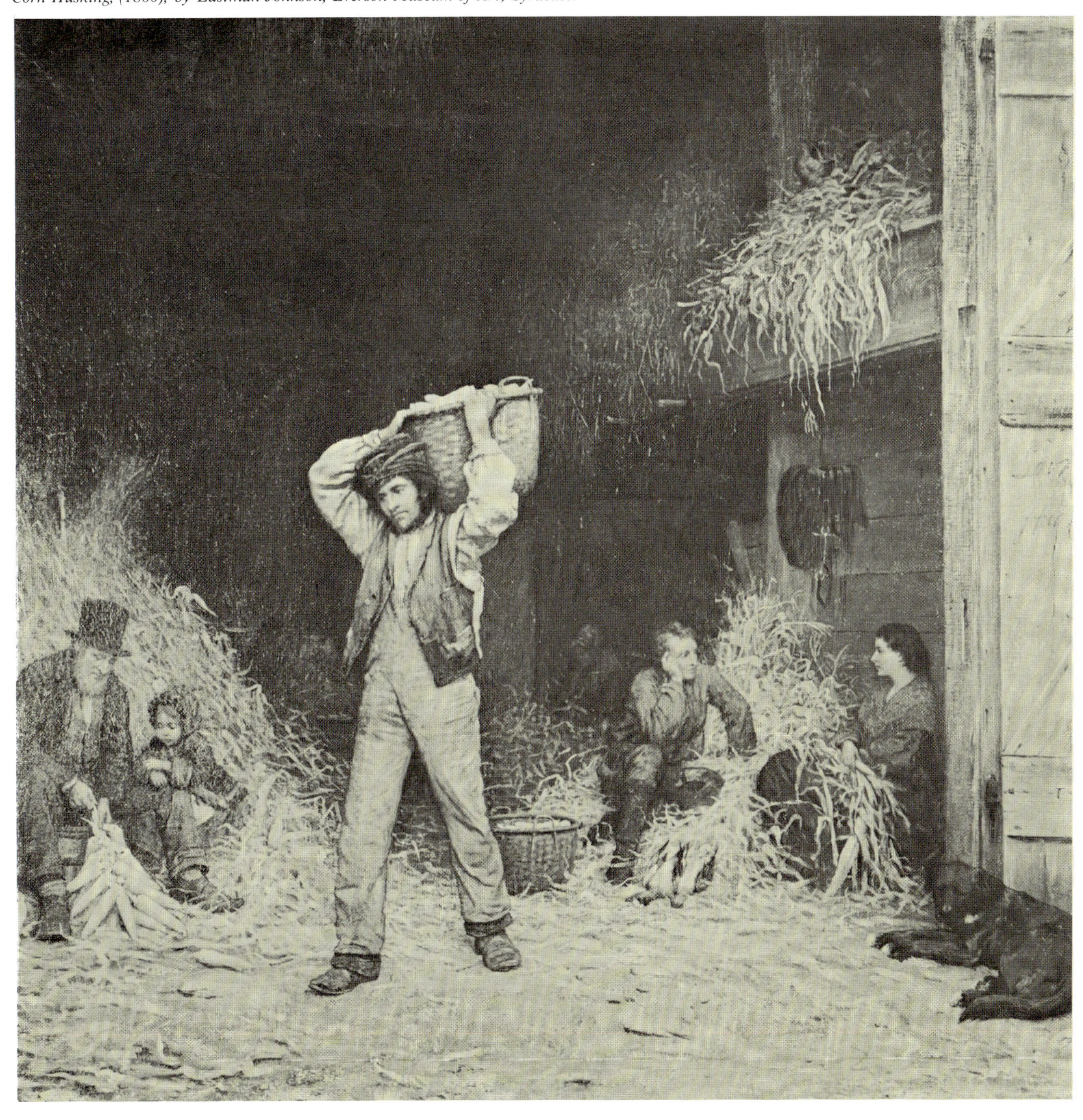

Contents

Introduction

The earth. Red, yellow, brown, and rich black earth. Man needs food to live. The earth is its source.

Once he hunted and fished, or picked wild fruits and berries to supply his needs. As his numbers increased this way of life became too unreliable to depend upon.

He turned to the soil and began to cultivate the earth. He prepared the ground, planted the seeds, tended the plants, and looked to heaven for the rain and the sun needed to give him a good harvest. He domesticated animals and turned from huntsman to herdsman and shepherd. But he had enemies: storm, frost, disease, locust, blight. Drought would parch his land, strangle his seeds, leave his animals to die and him and his family to hunger and misery. But in good times he would reap in joy the harvest of his labors and nature's blessing.

The farmers' work has been hard manual labor with primitive tools from dawn to sunset. Today, however, the burden of feeding the world is performed by fewer and fewer people, aided by remarkable machinery that lightens the farmer's labor and increases his ability to produce food.

This book will survey the farmer at work through the ages, and show how his labors have been depicted by the artist. Prehistoric man, who lived in caves before agricultural life began, painted wild bulls whose domesticated descendants inhabit our dairy farms and ranches today. Since the earliest times, man at work in his fields, or with his animals, has been a subject for artists. The tomb art of Egypt and China stressed agriculture in the belief that the food and laborers would serve a master in another world. There were long periods in art history when painting scenes of everyday life was unfashionable, but since the 17th and 18th centuries the artist has returned again and again to the farmer for his subject matter. Certain painters such as Pieter Brueghel the Elder and Jean Francois Millet devoted a large portion of their work to just this theme.

Here a contemporary of ours, Joán Miró, depicts a small farm of his native Spain. This is not a photographic likeness of any one place, but a painting that stresses the patterns and shapes that Miró noticed in the objects on a farm. The farmyard with its clutter of tools and implements, the stalk of corn, the furrows, the path to the well, the animal house, with roosters, hens, rabbits and a goat, are all there. The little farm grows scarce in our own country today, but it is still common in many places around the world.

Now let us look at the work of many artists in different times and see how they have portrayed the farmer doing his job.

The Farm, (1921-22); by Joán Miró, (1893-), With Permission from Mrs. Ernest Hemingway.

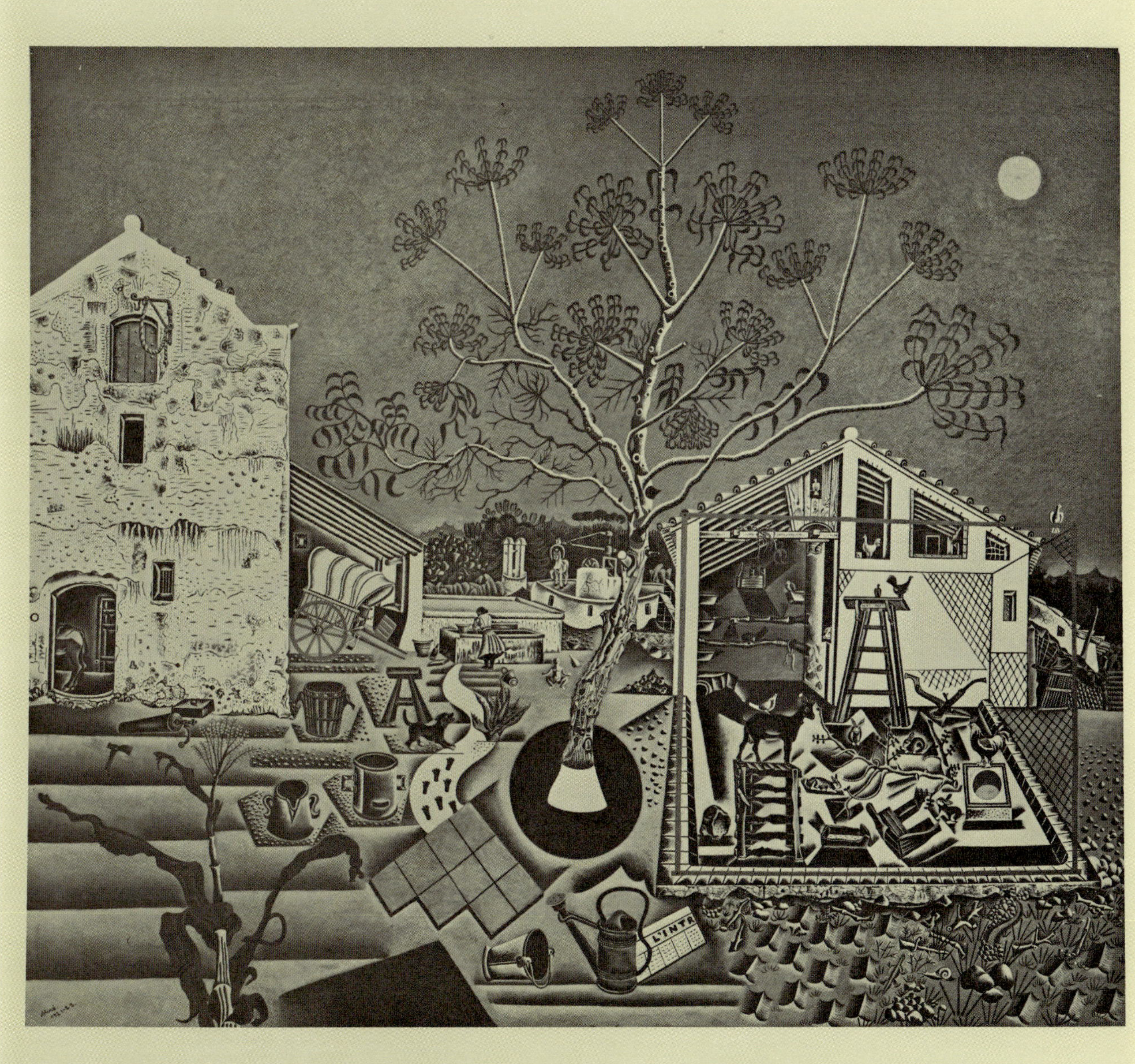

Officers of the Household of Sebkhotpe, Egyptian, (15th Century BC); Courtesy of the Oriental Institute, University of Chicago.

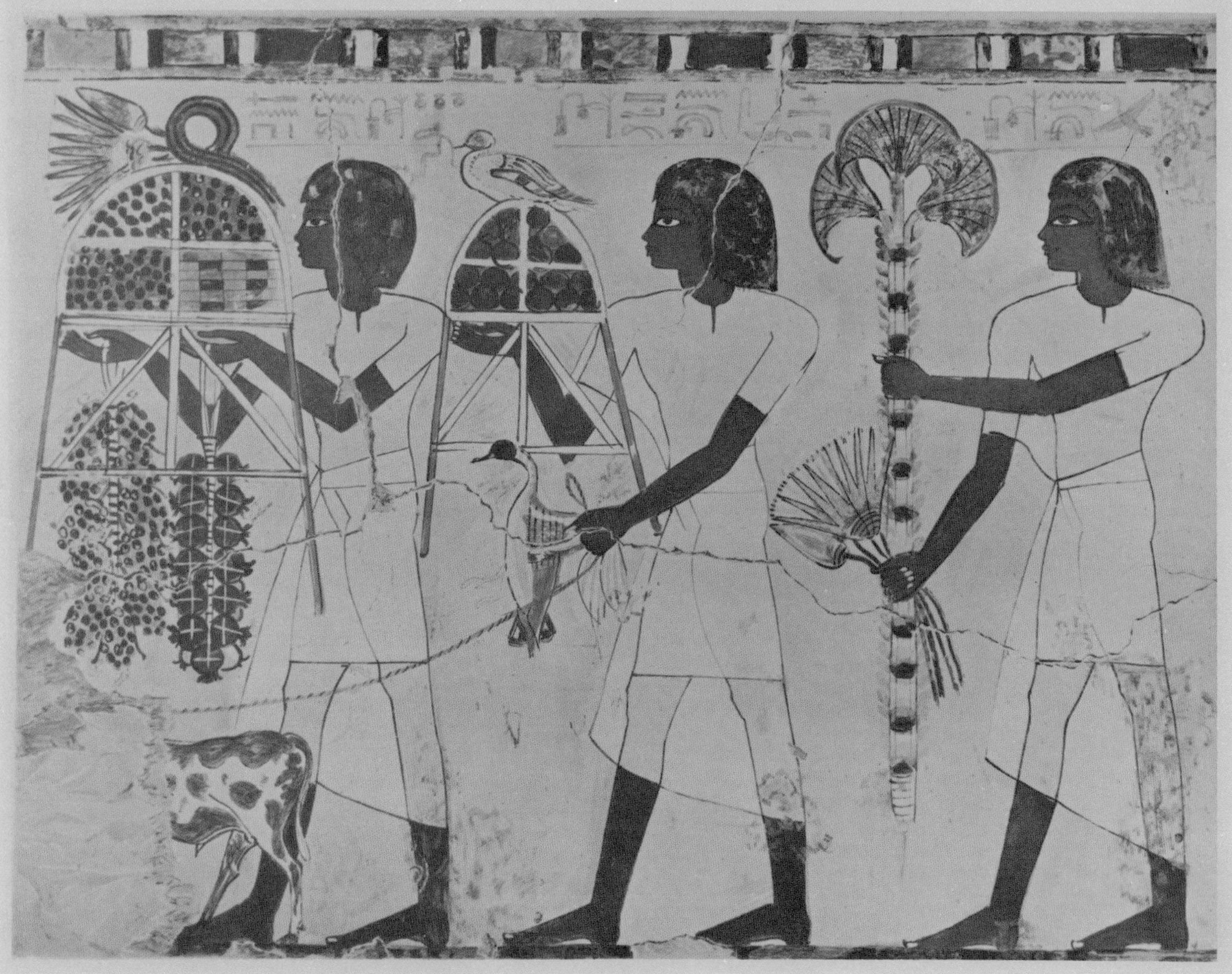

This Egyptian scene of the *Officers of the Household of Sebkhotpe* was painted about 3,400 years ago. It is a picture no one was supposed to see. These painted servants were intended to last forever, to provide Sebkhotpe with the necessities of life in the afterworld. The ancient Egyptians believed that after death all the normal needs of life would continue. Tombs were furnished with chairs, beds, dishes, food, weapons and tools. Wall paintings of grain fields, vineyards and models of wood or clay of men and animals who would do the work, were included. Religious and symbolic objects and paintings were also placed in the tombs. Some of the food carried in the painting, *Officers of the Household of Sebkhotpe,* might have been intended as offerings to the gods. In this picture the products of the farmer, the hunter and the herdsman are carried by the first two men. The third man carries lotus flowers and tall stalks of the *papyrus* plant. Papyrus was made into scrolls for writing.

The Egyptian artist did not draw objects in space exactly as we see them. He tried to show every object and action as clearly as possible by painting figures as if they were flattened, partly side-view and partly front-view.

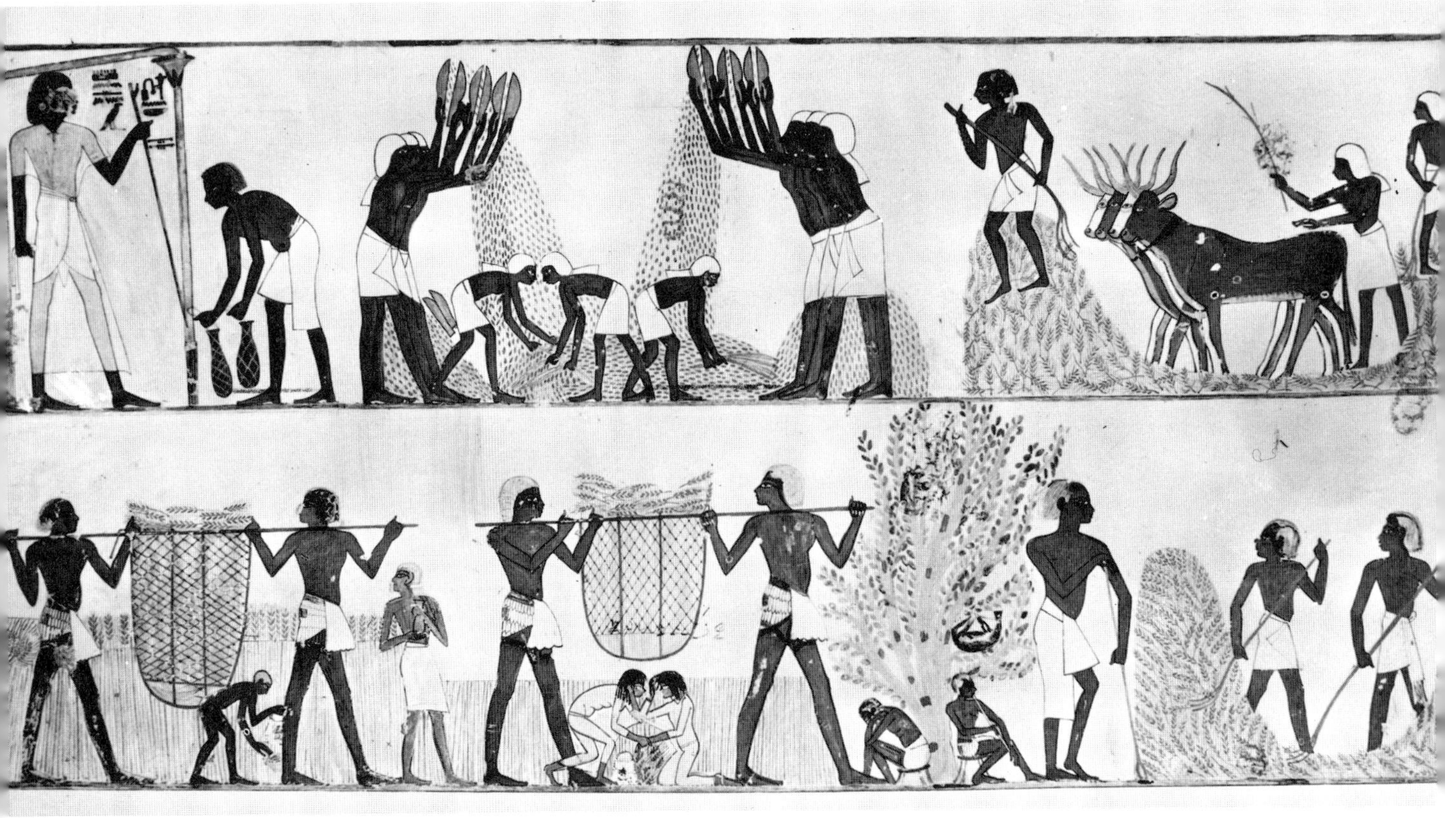

Harvest Scene, Egyptian, (15th Century BC); Courtesy of the Oriental Institute, University of Chicago.

At nearly the same time the *Officers of the Household of Sebkhotpe* was executed another Egyptian artist painted this *Harvest Scene* on the walls of the tomb of a nobleman named Menna. The painted harvesters were intended to provide food for the nobleman in the afterworld. Other pictures show the steps in growing grain, and as a result, we know a good deal about ancient Egyptian farming. The artist's thoroughness in showing each stage of the harvest makes this painting more useful than a written description might have been. You don't have to be able to read Egyptian *hieroglyphics* (HIRE-uh-GLIF-ics) to know what was going on.

The story starts at the lower left, where wheat is carried in huge baskets to the threshing floor. There an overseer leans on a staff while he supervises two laborers. Above, the story continues from right to left. Oxen trample the wheat to separate the grain from the stalks. Next, men winnow so that the husks can be blown away from the grain. The last scene, at the upper left, shows the overseer counting jars of grain. Perhaps he is doing this to figure out the landowner's share of the harvest. In many ways the harvesting of grain as seen here remained unchanged until the invention of modern farm machinery.

Ancient Egyptians cultivated the rich land along the banks of the Nile. Grain was their most important crop, and details of planting and harvest appear again and again in their art work. Much Egyptian art was preserved in tombs because of the Egyptian burial customs and belief in afterlife.

Here is another ancient Egyptian tomb painting depicting agriculture. *Peasants Driving Cattle and Fishing* is a shallow relief sculpture in stone. Look closely and you will see a waterline running all the way across the sculpture. The cattle are being driven through the water by herdsmen. They are walking along the river bottom.

The carving shows the cattle lightly overlapped, to indicate depth. But their hooves are placed along the same ground line because Egyptian artists did not use perspective. The horns, shown in front view, make a very handsome pattern of curving lines. Notice how one cow bends her head to the surface of the water to drink. The calf must be carried because the water would be too deep for it to walk through. Its mother reaches out to lick it. The fishermen, who are drawing a net full of fish from the water, suggest a series of actions. The entire scene is very lively, even though individual figures are posed stiffly. A feeling of movement almost like stop-motion photography is created by the repeated lines of the legs of both men and cattle.

Originally this sculpture was painted in bright colors. But nearly all the color has flaked away except for the reddish tan of the fishermen's legs. A painting made with water paint on stone is not very durable. As long as an Egyptian tomb remained sealed, the paintings were preserved. But when the tomb was opened, the changes in temperature and moisture in the air made the paint flake off the pictures. If this painting had not been made on a carving in stone, most of the picture would have been lost.

Egyptian artists used the earth colors yellow and red ochre, the mineral colors blue and green, carbon black from soot, and chalk white. These were mixed with water to get a paint very much like our tempera.

Peasants Driving Cattle and Fishing, Egyptian, (2560-2420 BC); Detroit Institute of Arts.

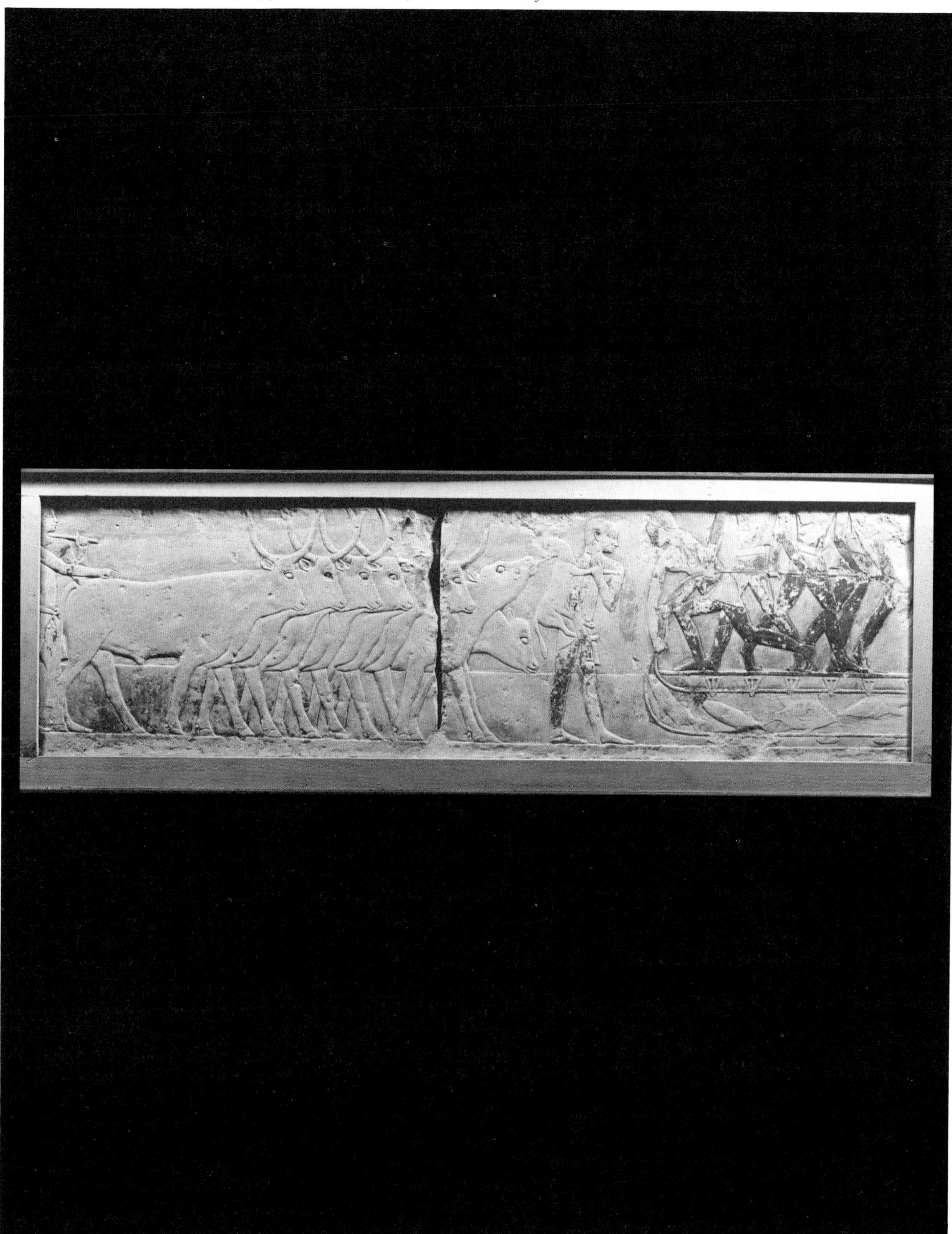

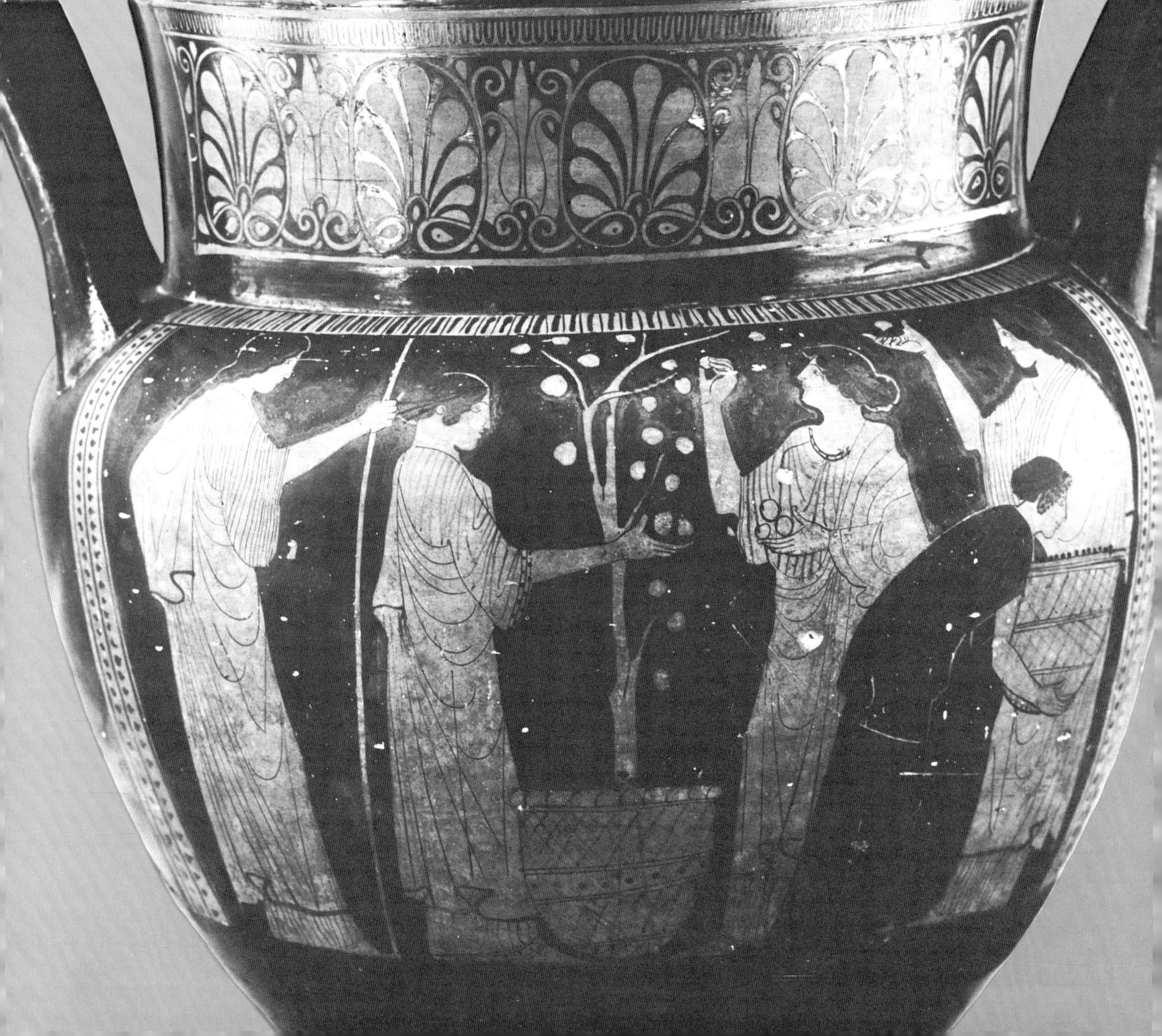

In *Women Picking Apples* one can see the freedom with which Greek artists drew the human figure. The women are shown working in an orchard, but the artist allowed room for only one tree in the design. Notice how the apple tree looks almost as if it were growing out of the basket into which the apples are being placed. The Egyptians followed strict rules and avoided this confusion by showing objects side by side instead of overlapping.

The paintings found on Greek ceramic vases, bottles and jars are very important because no other ancient Greek paintings have survived. Many of the containers were decorated with subjects from the Greek myths. A great number also show scenes from daily life. Unlike the paintings in Egyptian tombs, intended for the afterworld, these paintings decorated objects that were to be used every day. One might enjoy a picture while drinking from a shallow bowl or while pouring oil from a slender bottle. Vases were made in a specific shape and size for each different purpose.

The Orchard Vase, Detail, Greek, (about 460 BC); The Metropolitan Museum of Art, Rogers Fund, 1907.

A duck pond was one of the usual features of a Chinese farm. The ducks were not only pleasant to watch, but like any domesticated fowl, they would end up on the dinner table.

The Chinese, in common with the Egyptians, wished to provide their dead with provisions for afterlife. During the Han (hahn) period in China, 2,000 years ago, it was customary to place clothing, furniture, jewelry, useful objects and small sculptures into the tombs. Among the most interesting items were ceramic (suh-RAM-ic) figures of animals and buildings, representing the person's property. Sometimes a group of farm animals, birds, and buildings would be made with a wall around it, as if an entire farmyard were to be represented.

This sculptured *Duck Pond* was produced from clay, covered with a very thin glaze and *fired*, or baked, at a high temperature. The artist who made this group was quite realistic. He showed various sizes of ducks. There is even one in the water fluttering its wings as if to fly away.

Duck Pond, Chinese, (206 BC-221 AD); Chicago Natural History Museum.

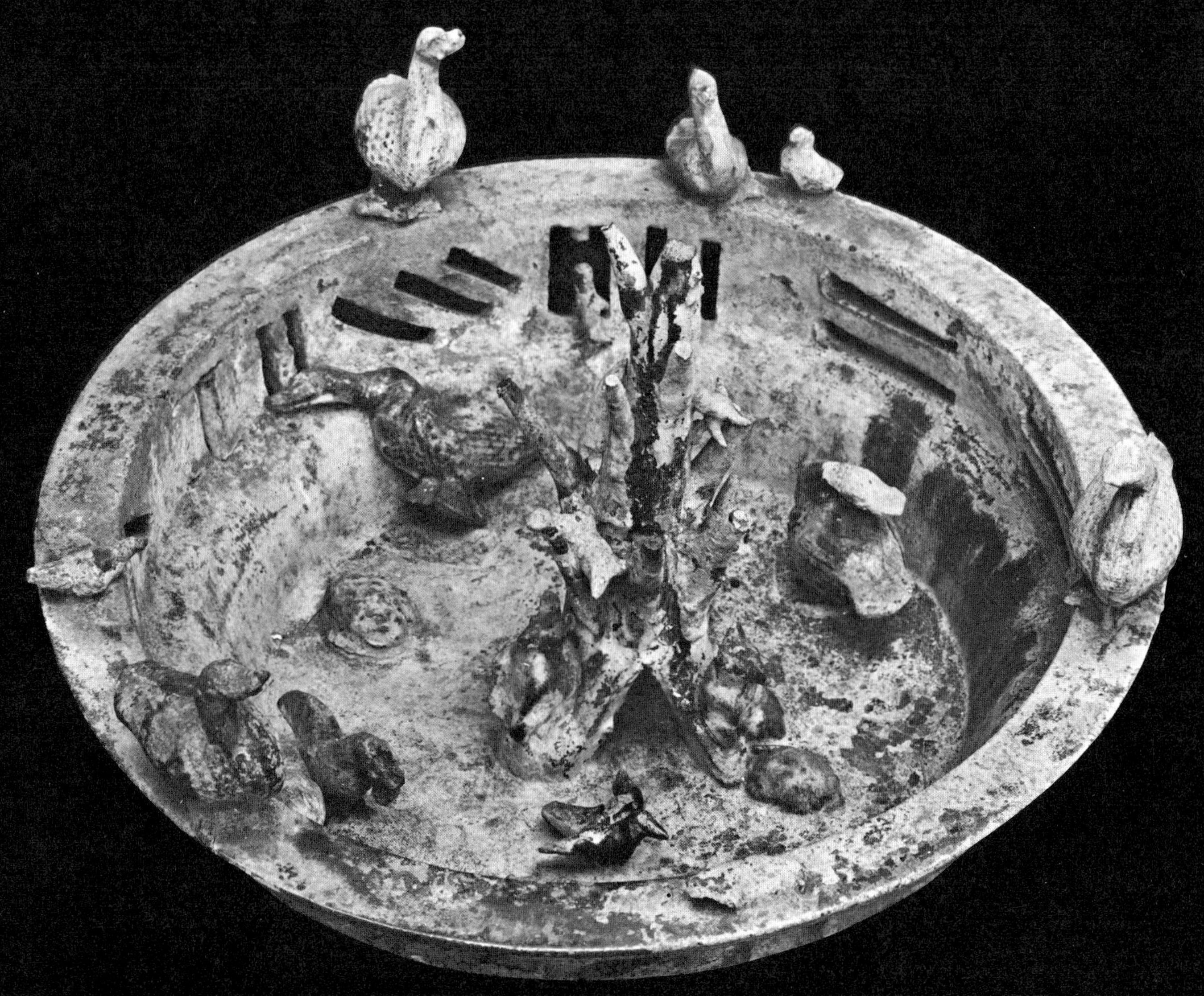

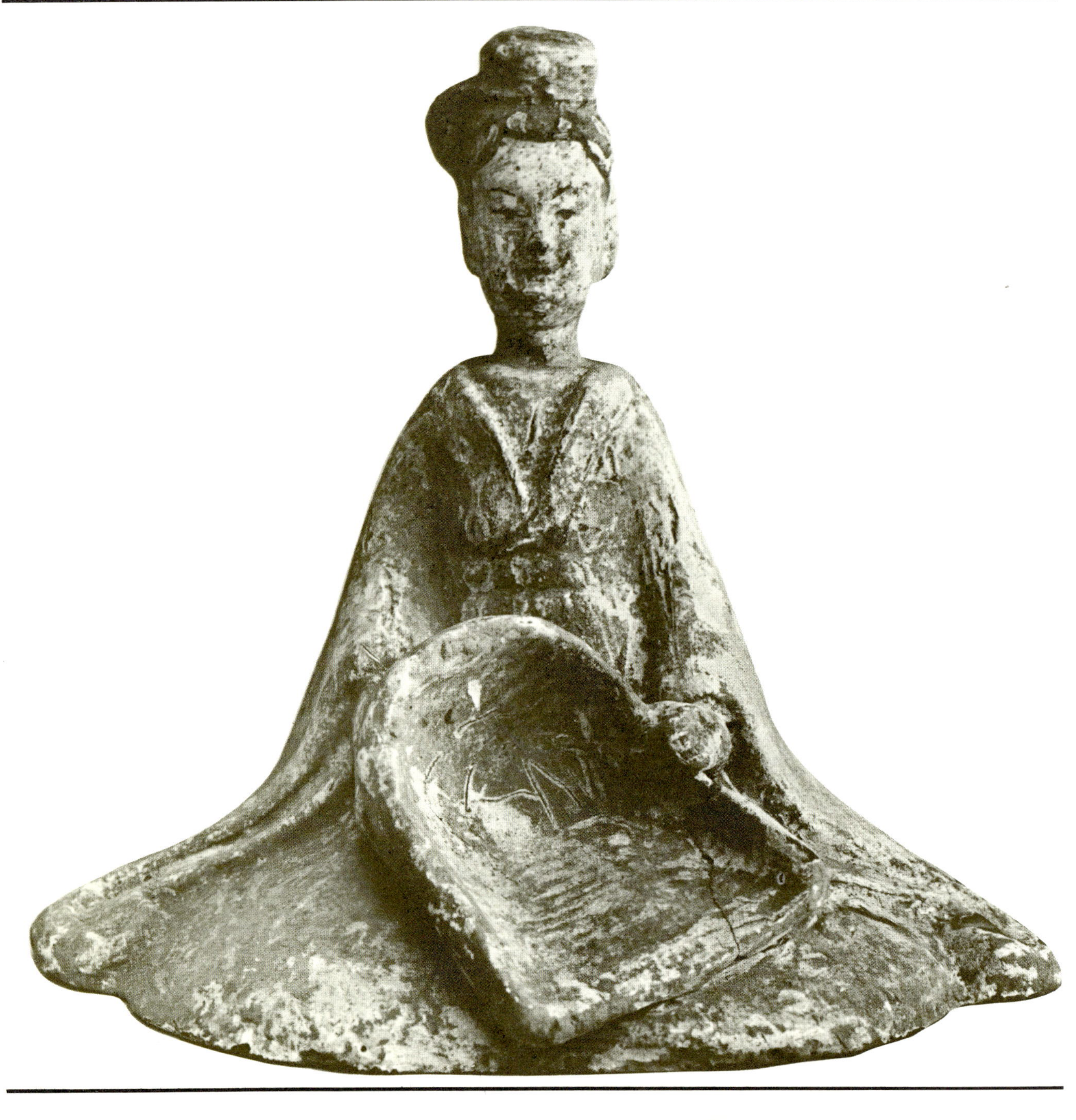

This *Girl with Harvesting Instrument* is another Chinese tomb figure. She is seated with her long flowing robe spread about her. Her hair is piled high in an elegant arrangement. It is difficult to be certain just what she is holding, but it may be a basket for winnowing grain. The clay figure was painted after it was fired, and much of the paint has worn off.

This small figure may have represented one of a group of servants attending the person in whose tomb the figures were placed. She seems like a far more charming companion for the afterworld than some of the rather stiff Egyptian figures we have seen. Don't you agree?

The Chinese tomb never seems to have been an imposing building as was the Egyptian pyramid. It often was covered with earth to make an artificial hill. We do not have examples of all the objects buried in Chinese tombs, because China's severe weather conditions tended to destroy buried paintings, fabrics and wood. Only stone, metal, and fired clay, or ceramic objects were able to survive long burial. These small tomb sculptures help us to understand how people lived on farms in ancient China.

Girl With Harvesting Instrument, Chinese, (3rd-7th Century AD); The Metropolitan Museum of Art, New York, Rogers Fund.

The Good Shepherd is a mosaic wall decoration from an early Christian tomb. The Christian church had become the main patron of the arts. Religious figures and scenes from the Bible were needed to decorate churches and chapels. If subjects of everyday life were painted, it was because they were related to religious themes. For example, carpenters might be shown at work building Noah's Ark. Or, stone masons might be shown building the tower of Babel. Farmers might be shown in connection with some of the parables of Christ.

Everyday subjects like these were infrequent, but religious ideas were often symbolized by experiences familiar to everyone. Sometimes Christ was represented by a shepherd watching over his flock. This was true especially in the early days of the Church, when people were reluctant to create an image of Christ.

Here the shepherd and sheep are used as symbols. There is only a token landscape of a few rocks and leaves. The figure and animals look solid. Their forms are simplified and rather flat. The mosaic technique of making a picture by placing small colored stones and pieces of glass in cement encouraged this tendency toward flatness.

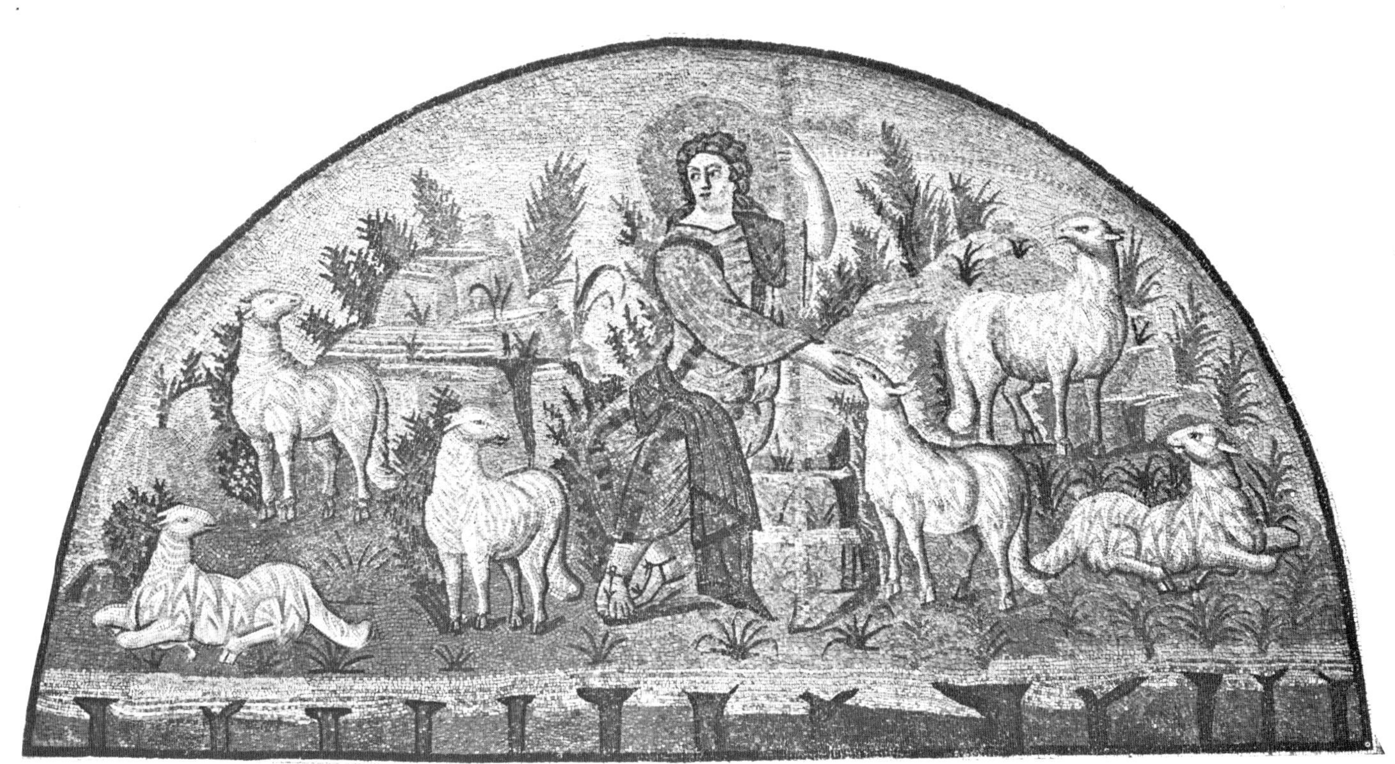

The Good Shepherd, Italian, artist unknown, (about 450 AD); The Mausoleum of Galla Placidia, Ravenna; Photo Alinari.

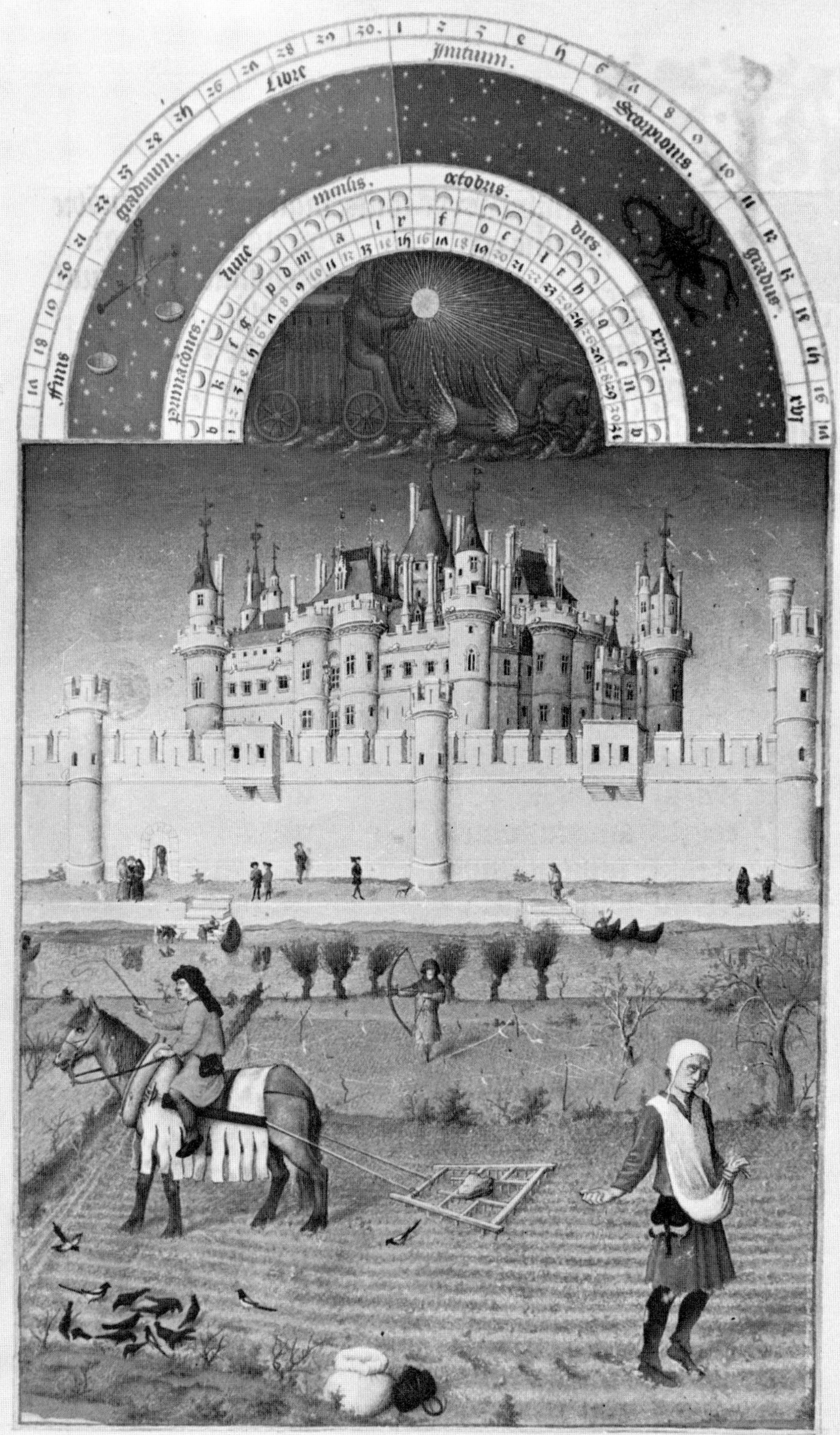

During the Middle Ages, before the invention of the printing press, books were lettered by hand. Decorations were often painted in the margins, and capital letters were interwoven with pictures or designs. This was called *illumination.* Sometimes full-page illustrations showing biblical events or episodes from the lives of the saints were included.

Prayerbooks also contained a calendar as a guide to worship. The most famous of these calendars is in *The Very Rich Book of Hours* by Pol de Limbourg. The book was owned by Jean de Berry, who was a younger brother of the French king and a great patron of the arts.

Each illustration in the calendar shows activities appropriate to the month, as they took place on one of the duke's estates. March depicts plowing; June, haymaking; July, the harvest; August, a falcon hunt, the harvest continuing, and men swimming in a river. The Duke de Berry is shown dining with his courtiers during the cold month of January. *The Month of October,* which you see here, contains a man on horseback harrowing to level the land and break up clods of soil. Another man sows winter wheat. Birds have gathered in the foreground to eat the seed, but they seem to have been frightened away from the other field by the archer-scarecrow.

The castle in the background, the early Louvre in Paris, was one of the duke's properties. Farming of the castle lands was done by serfs. Times were troubled during the Middle Ages, and during attacks the serfs would seek shelter behind the walls of their lord's castle-fortress. They also had to fight in the lord's army. The serfs were considered unimportant people and their activities were not usually given such a prominent place in paintings at that time.

The realism of Pol de Limbourg's painting was also unusual. He showed depth fairly successfully, although he filled the page with a design which cut off any distant view. Most artists of his time still painted a landscape as if it were tilted upward.

Pol de Limbourg and his brothers were all painters who worked for Jean de Berry. They painted beautiful illustrations for many books the duke commissioned. You can see how costly these books would be. Only a royal prince could afford such treasures.

The Very Rich Book of Hours of the Duke de Berry, (1411-16); by Pol de Limbourg, (? -1416), Musee Conde, Chantilly; Photo Giraudon.

A calendar certainly doesn't cover an entire wall in today's homes. But that is precisely what the tapestry *September* did. It is one of a series showing the twelve months of the year. Tapestries are woven hangings that were used during the Middle Ages as wall decorations. They also served to cover the cold stone walls of the castles and keep out the drafts. Unlike the decorations which were often painted on the walls, tapestries could be packed in chests to be moved from one castle to another, so that the owner could enjoy his favorites wherever he lived.

In *September* the grape harvest is shown. Bacchus, the god of wine, watches it from above. The gathering of grapes takes place in the background. The most important activity occurs in the center of the tapestry, where men are treading on the grapes to squeeze the juice for wine. A circle showing the months and the signs of the zodiac encloses the main picture. Watching the entire scene from the upper corners of the tapestry are Jupiter and Semele, the parents of Bacchus. Notice the names near the figures of the gods.

The entire tapestry is crowded with detail and rich ornamentation. Nearly all of the activity seems close to the surface. This kind of design emphasizes the flatness and solidity of the wall it is made to decorate.

September, Flemish, (16th Century); Attributed to Bernard Van Orley, (1488-1582), The Minneapolis Institute of Arts.

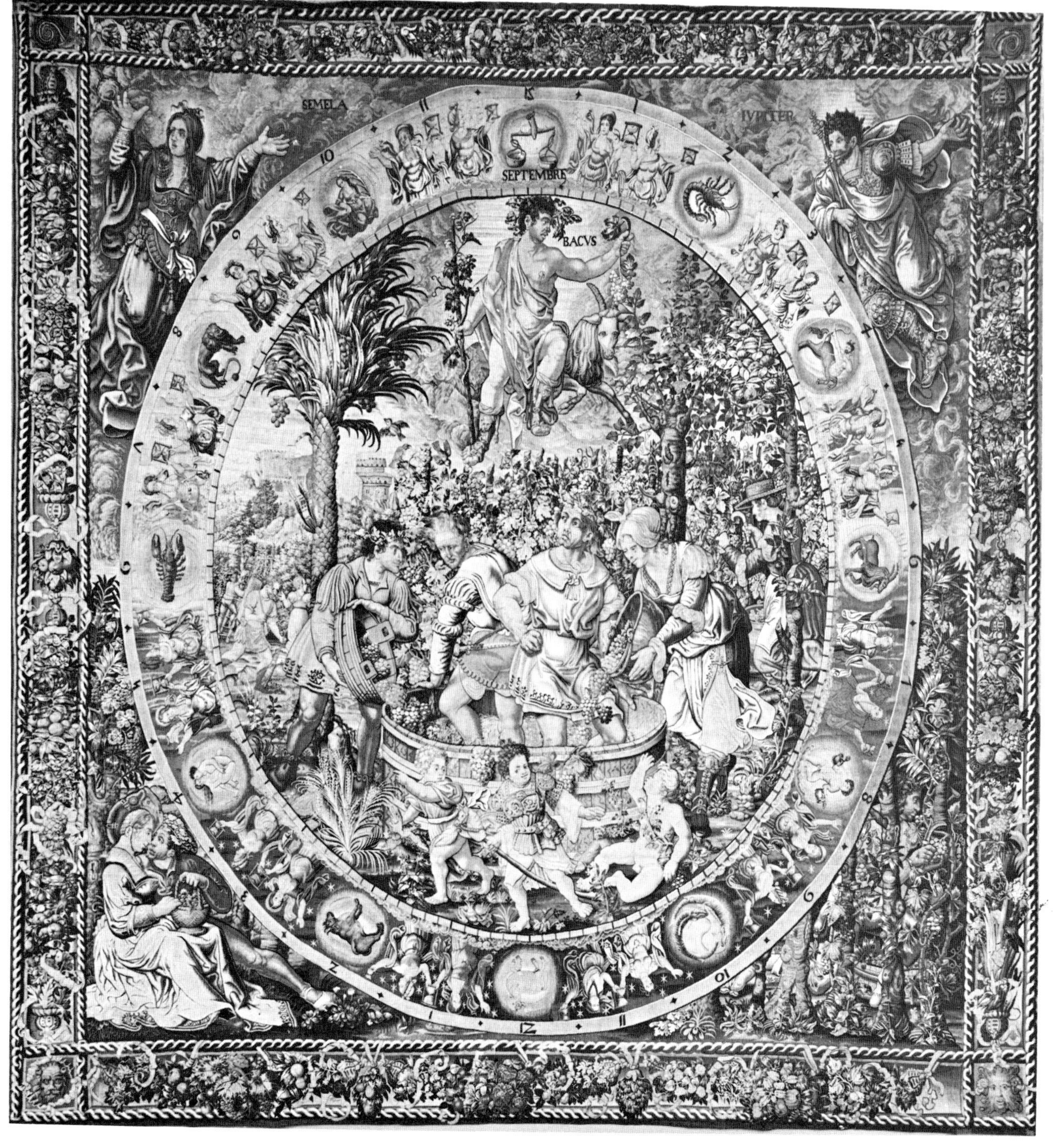
SEMELA
IVPITER
SEPTEMBRE
BACVS

During the Middle Ages in Europe most artists painted religious subjects. If landscapes or scenes of everyday life were included in a background, these would form only a small part of the picture. However, during the 15th century interest in science and all aspects of the natural world increased. Careful studies of landscapes were made by painters using new rules for realistic representation. A way of painting deep space from normal eye level was developed. It replaced the flattened and tilted bird's-eye view used in the Middle Ages.

Fra Bartolommeo (frah bar-tol-oh-MAY-oh) was a monk at the convent of San Marco in Florence. He painted religious subjects, but like most artists of his time, he made landscape studies as well. This pen-and-ink drawing of the Italian farmhouse is one of them. Drawn from a position on the road below the farm, it shows distant views to each side of the farmhouse. There is a continuous sense of depth because objects overlap and are shown smaller in the distance. This is a great change from the Egyptian style in which there is no attempt at all to show distance.

Farm on the Slope of a Hill, by Fra Bartolommeo, (1472-1517); The Cleveland Museum of Art; Gift of Hanna Fund, Delia E. and L. E. Holden Funds and Dudley P. Allen Fund.

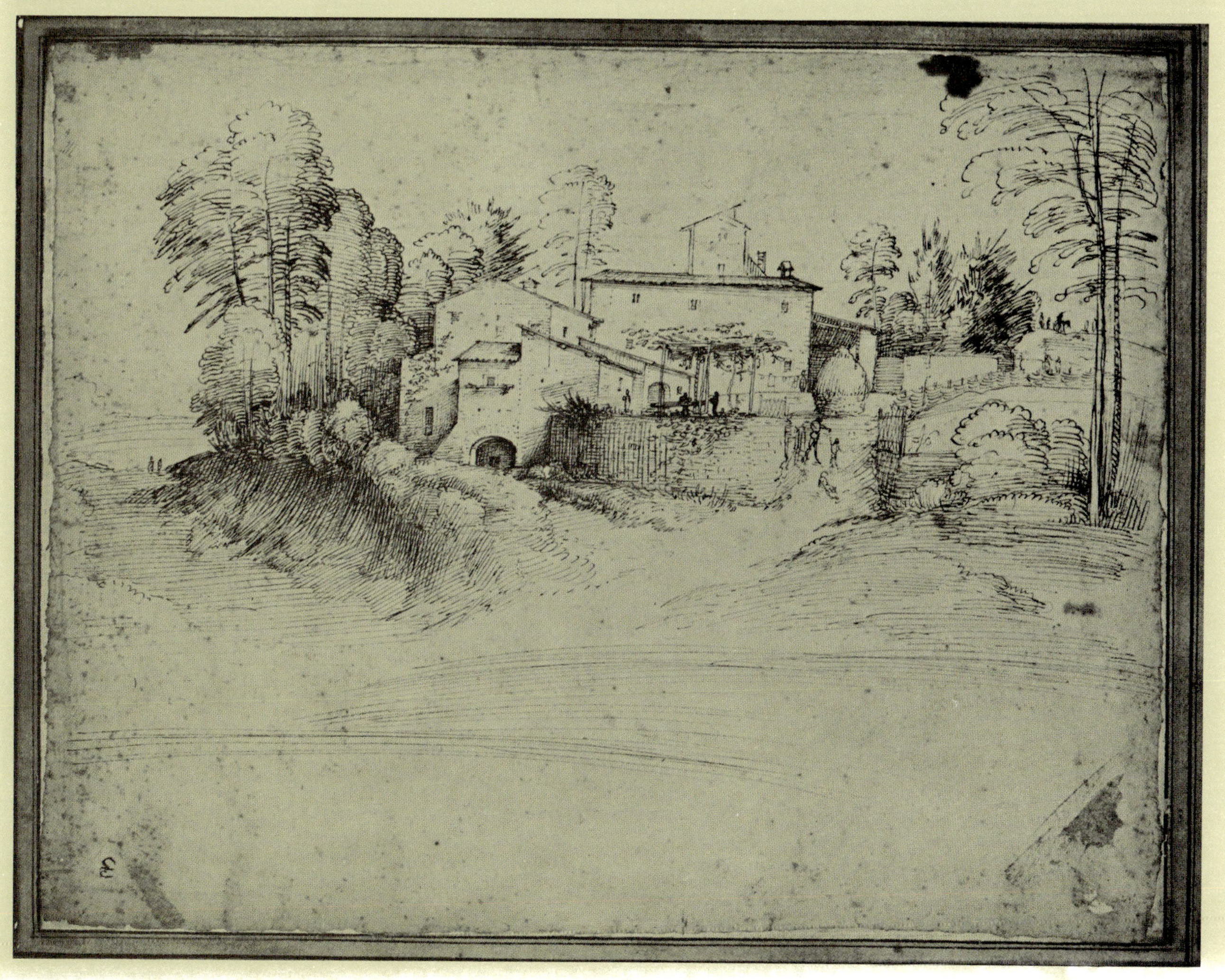

Rest on the Flight into Egypt illustrates a popular legend about the flight of the Holy Family from King Herod's soldiers. It tells how some of Herod's men, searching for Jesus, were fooled by a miracle. The painting shows several events taking place at the same time. Joseph fills a water flask at the spring to the left, while Mary and Jesus rest. In the distant village soldiers seek out and kill infants according to King Herod's command. Other soldiers ask a farmer whether he has seen the Holy Family. According to the legend, Jesus had told the farmer to say that he had seen them when he plowed his field. This field grew miraculously overnight, to make the soldiers believe that the farmer had plowed many weeks earlier and that the Holy Family had long since gone. We see that the other farmers are still plowing.

Patinir painted several versions of this subject. In them the Flemish artist demonstrated his ability as a fine landscape painter. He could not paint people so skillfully, and fellow artists sometimes added important figures to a painting for him. This kind of cooperation on a painting was quite common at that time. Although the connection of the foreground to the rest of the landscape is not very smooth, Patinir painted deep space according to the new rules. A quiet river valley, villages, towns, mountains, and woods stretch evenly to the horizon.

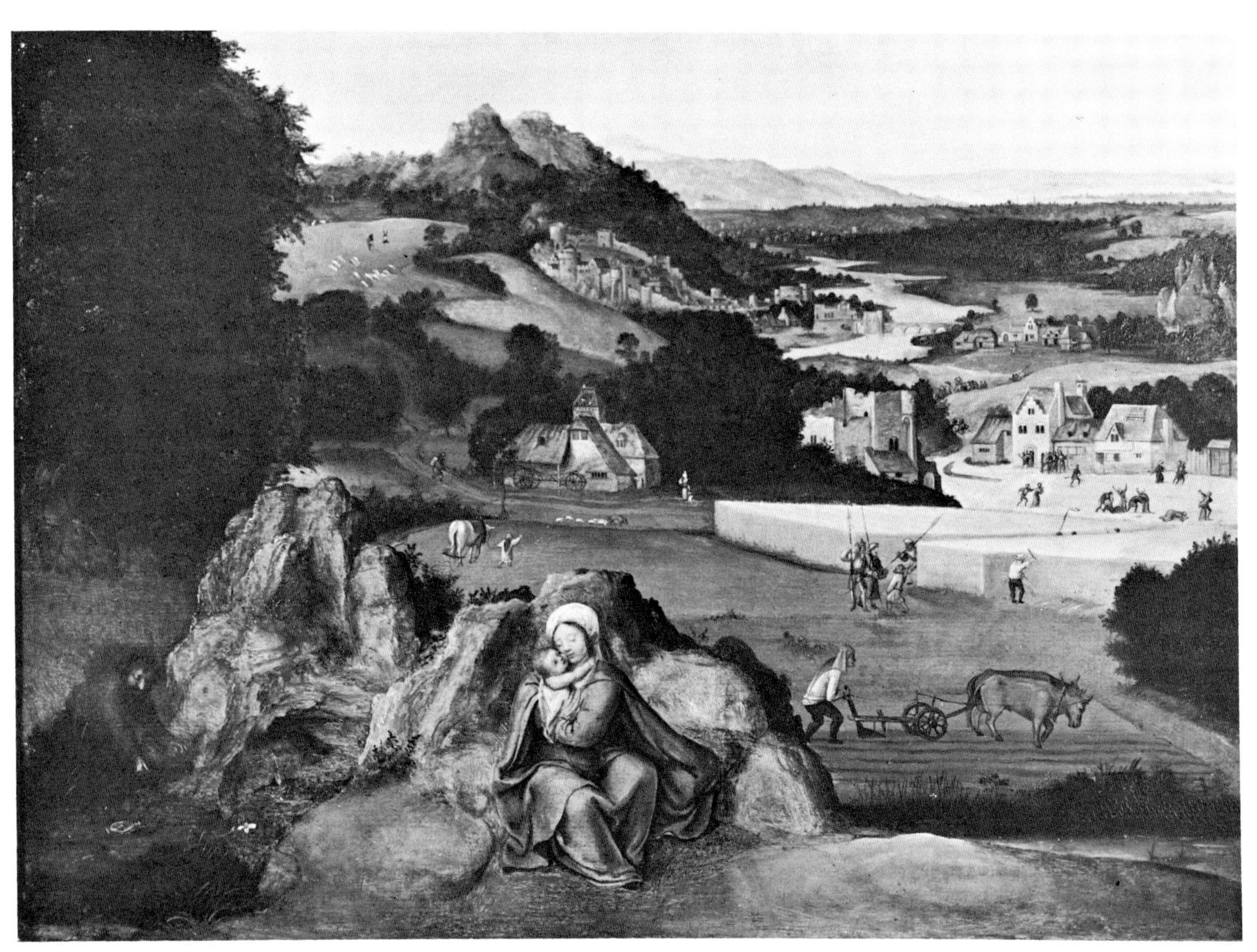

Rest on the Flight Into Egypt, by Joachim Patinir, (about 1480-1524); The Minneapolis Institute of Arts.

Pieter Brueghel (BREW-gul) the Elder, a Flemish artist, made the pen-and-ink drawing *Spring* in order to have it reproduced as a print for people who could not afford paintings for their homes. It shows nearly every activity of the season. The subject would be likely to appeal to almost everyone. The change of seasons has always been most important to the farmer. His daily work was determined for him by the time of the year. In this picture a farmer would find many familiar activities: digging in the garden, planting, trimming the grape vines, shearing sheep, and taking a moment off to enjoy a lovely Spring day.

Pieter Brueghel was able to show continuous movement through his picture from the foreground to the distant horizon. Italian painters were the first to work out methods for showing depth. Brueghel learned these methods when he went from his native Flanders to Italy to study. He was adept at drawing people in action. The man digging with a spade really bears down on it with all his weight. Men kneel and bend with a great deal of energy. The figures are solid and move freely. Brueghel could skillfully show many things going on in one uncrowded picture.

Spring, by Pieter Brueghel the Elder, (1525/30-1569); The Albertina, Vienna.

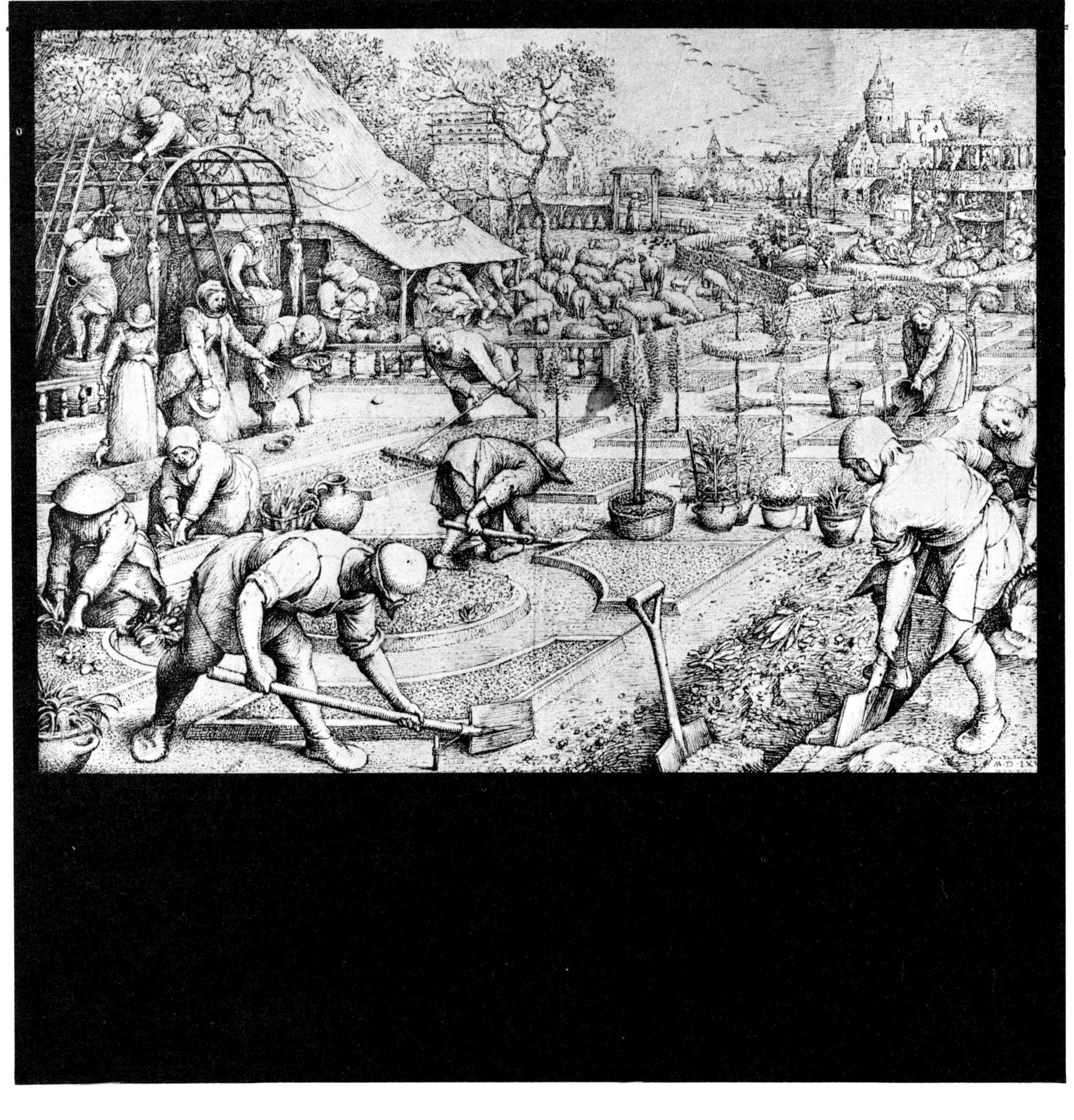

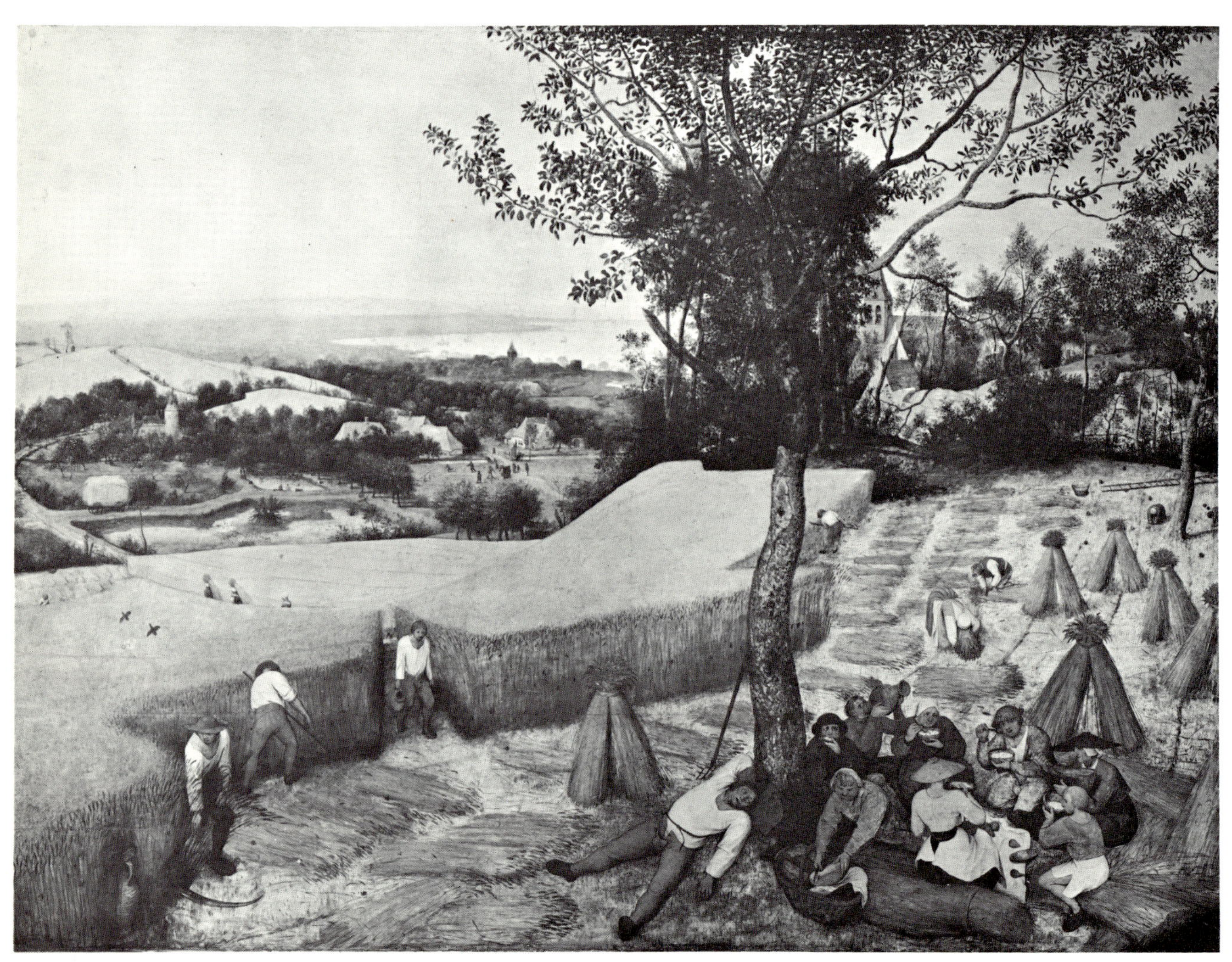

The Harvesters, (1565); by Pieter Brueghel the Elder, The Metropolitan Museum of Art, Rogers Fund, 1919.

At the end of summer, harvesting occupies the full energies and time of the farmer. The chores have to be completed quickly, and farmers work from dawn to dusk. Here we see three men working in the warm sun, reaping with long scythes while others gather the wheat into sheaves. In the far distance a hay wagon is piled high. The rest, including women and children, have stopped for a midday meal in the shade of a large tree. Huge loaves of bread are sliced to be eaten with bowls of curds and whey. There are pears for dessert, and more fruit is being gathered by children in the background.

When you look at this painting your eye may quickly take in the arrangement of trees, the rows of cut grain, and the figures in action. But Brueghel's picture is the result of many careful stages from first sketches to the finished oil painting. It is carefully organized so that everything going on may easily be seen as part of the whole. The path cut through the grain leads your eye beyond the road to more wheat fields. The curving movement continues to the village where the farmers live, and to harbors and towns in the distance. The zigzag diagonal of the wheat being cut and the large tree divide the painting into areas of closeness and distance. Through the trees at the right parts of a nearby church are visible. Stacks of wheat act like little arrows pointing upward, to help unite the upper and lower parts of the painting. Throughout, *The Harvesters* is dominated by the glow of the ripe, golden wheat.

The Team of Horses, by Pieter Brueghel the Elder; The Albertina, Vienna.

The drawing of *The Team of Horses* is an example of the kind of careful study Pieter Brueghel made of his peasant subjects. He drew with pen and brownish ink, and made notations about color in various parts of the figures. His observant eye picked out every detail: how the horse's harness was put together, the braided tip of the horse's tail, how the man's jacket was made, and even the elbow patch on his sleeve. Brueghel didn't shade his drawing completely. Instead, he indicated the roundness of the horse's body and its bony structure with short lines and dots. He took great care, however, in drawing the eye of the horse on the far side, as if he wanted to be sure that he would remember how to paint it later.

Brueghel often attended village weddings and other festivities, as well as simply observing day-to-day farm and village life. Wherever he found an interesting subject he would make a study like this one. Some of these he labeled as being drawn from life to emphasize the accuracy of his drawings and to distinguish them from those done from memory. Along with his paintings, they form a fascinating record of the customs and dress of the 16th century.

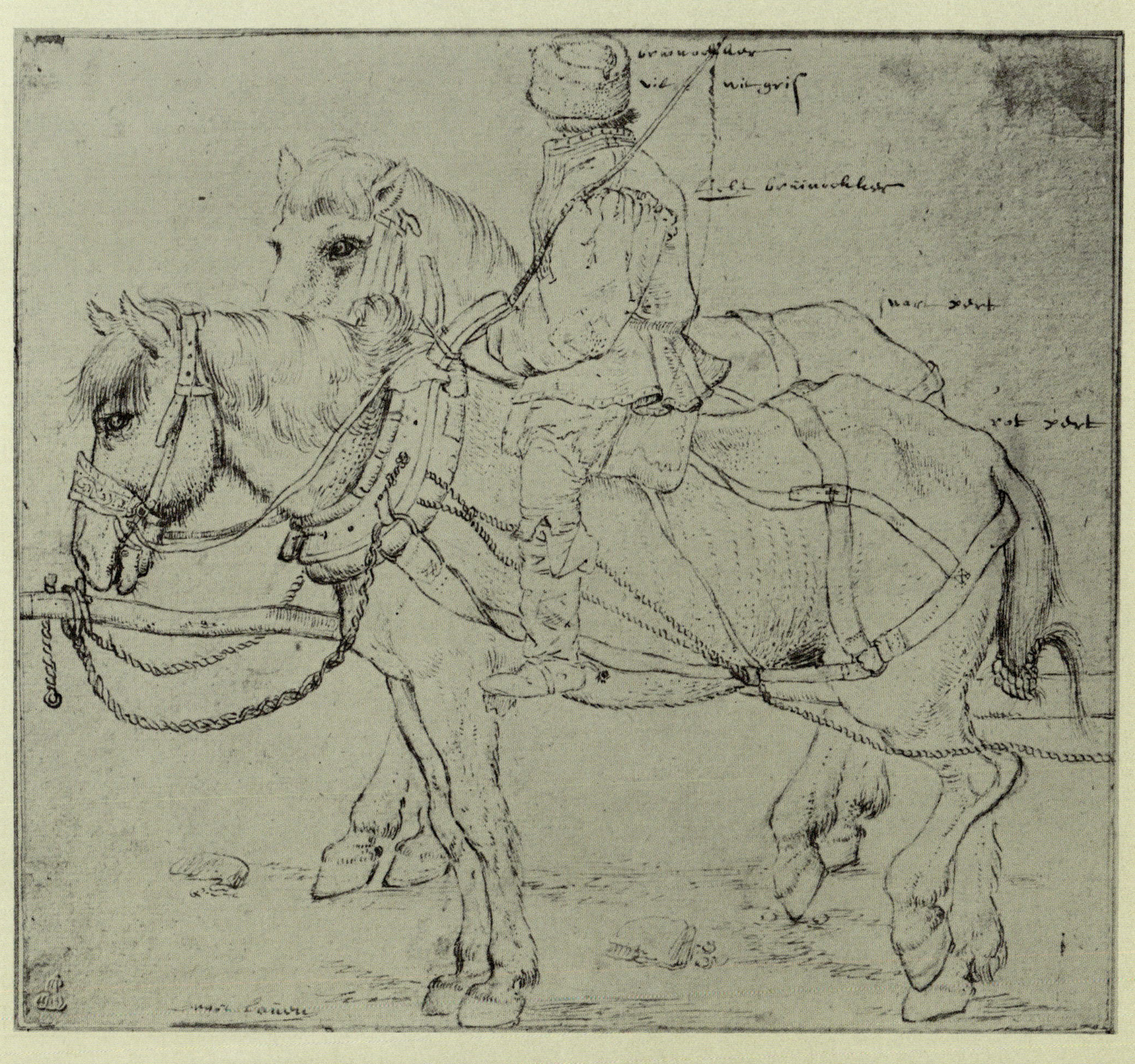

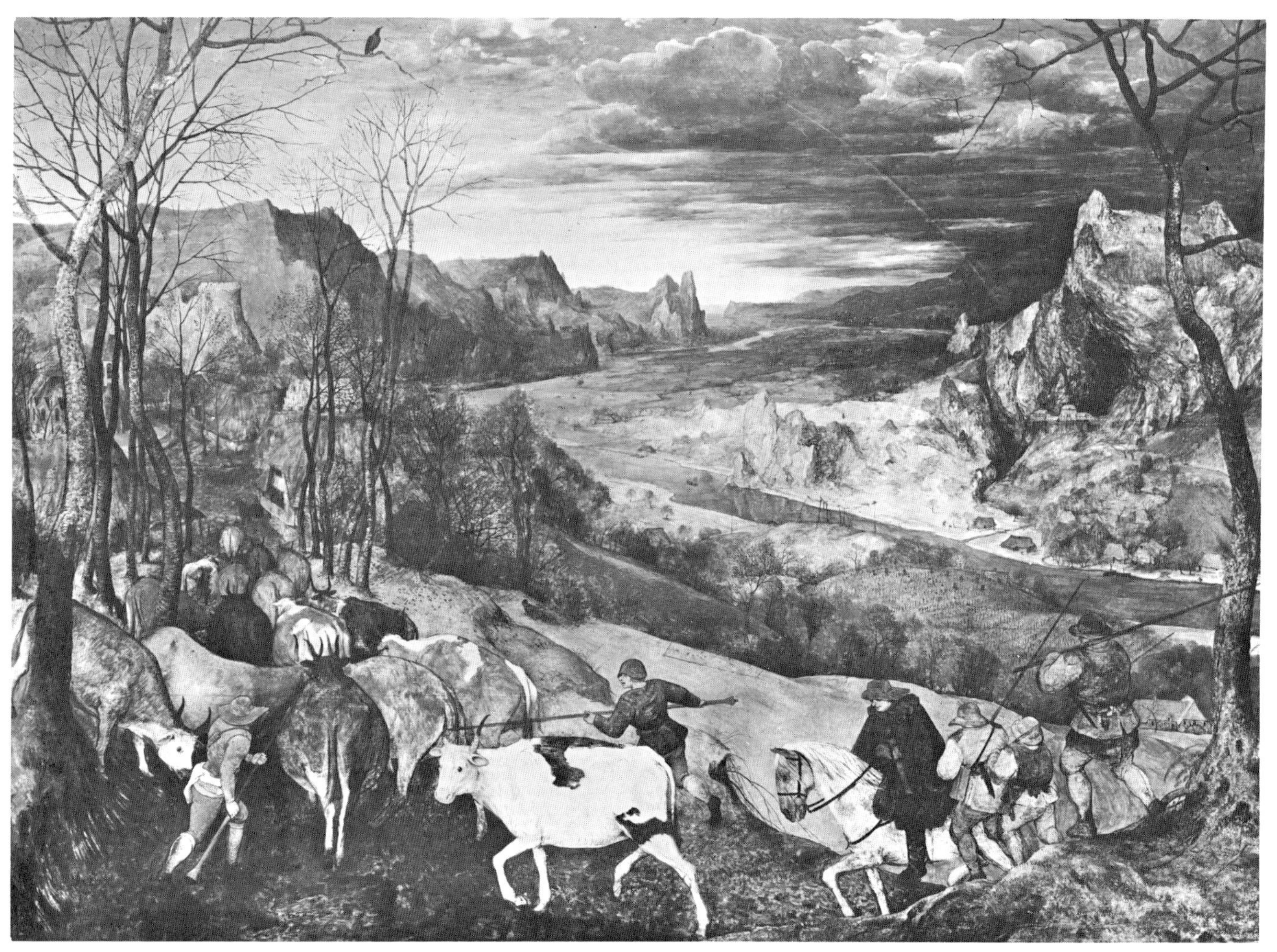

The Return of the Herd, (1565); by Pieter Brueghel the Elder, Kunsthistorischen Museum, Vienna.

As winter approaches and the days become shorter the cattle must be brought down from summer pastures to the village. The farmers, bundled up against the chill, suggest the coming winter. Slowly the cattle are herded together and led down the path.

The landscape which forms the important part of this painting, *The Return of the Herd,* is not entirely realistic. This is surprising because we have seen the care that Pieter Brueghel took in painting peasant life, and his concern for realism and accurate detail. As a young man Brueghel had travelled from Flanders to Italy in order to study Italian art. When he passed through the Alps he was impressed by the wild and rugged beauty of these mountains. When he painted the mountains or hills of his native land, he drew from his memory of the Alps. He sometimes exaggerated the Flemish landscape and made it seem far wilder and more fantastic in his paintings than it really was. Some of the drawings made on his travels may have been the basis for the rocky cliffs and rugged peaks in this picture.

Brueghel loved to paint vast stretches of landscape. He was impressed by the endless wonder of creation. One feels the power of nature in the dark, ominous clouds. There is a threatening feeling in the strong, twisting form of the mountain at the right. The farmers and their village are confronted with the vastness of the river valley, mountains and sky.

The little girl holds out her apron to catch the apples her brother is knocking down. Two other children are wrestling on the ground. A sow is busy feeding and pays no attention to them. The Flemish artist Abraham Bloemaert (BLOOM-ehrt), intended this picture to be a landscape study of trees and farm buildings. However, he must have enjoyed watching the children, so he included them in the picture. Perhaps he thought they would make the lower left hand part of his picture more lively. It certainly would seem rather empty without them.

A thatch-roofed barn and a storage building on stilts have curious, irregular shapes. They are drawn with the same short curving lines that Bloemaert used for describing the bank of the stream, the low wall, the trees, and the rickety gate. The pen-and-ink lines are cross-hatched here and there for darker shadows. Instead of color, lines alone show all the changes in light, texture and shapes. Overlapping, twisting and looping, the lines weave in and out and lead your eye to explore one area of the picture after another.

Farmstead Under Trees With Children Playing, by Abraham Bloemaert, (1564-1651).

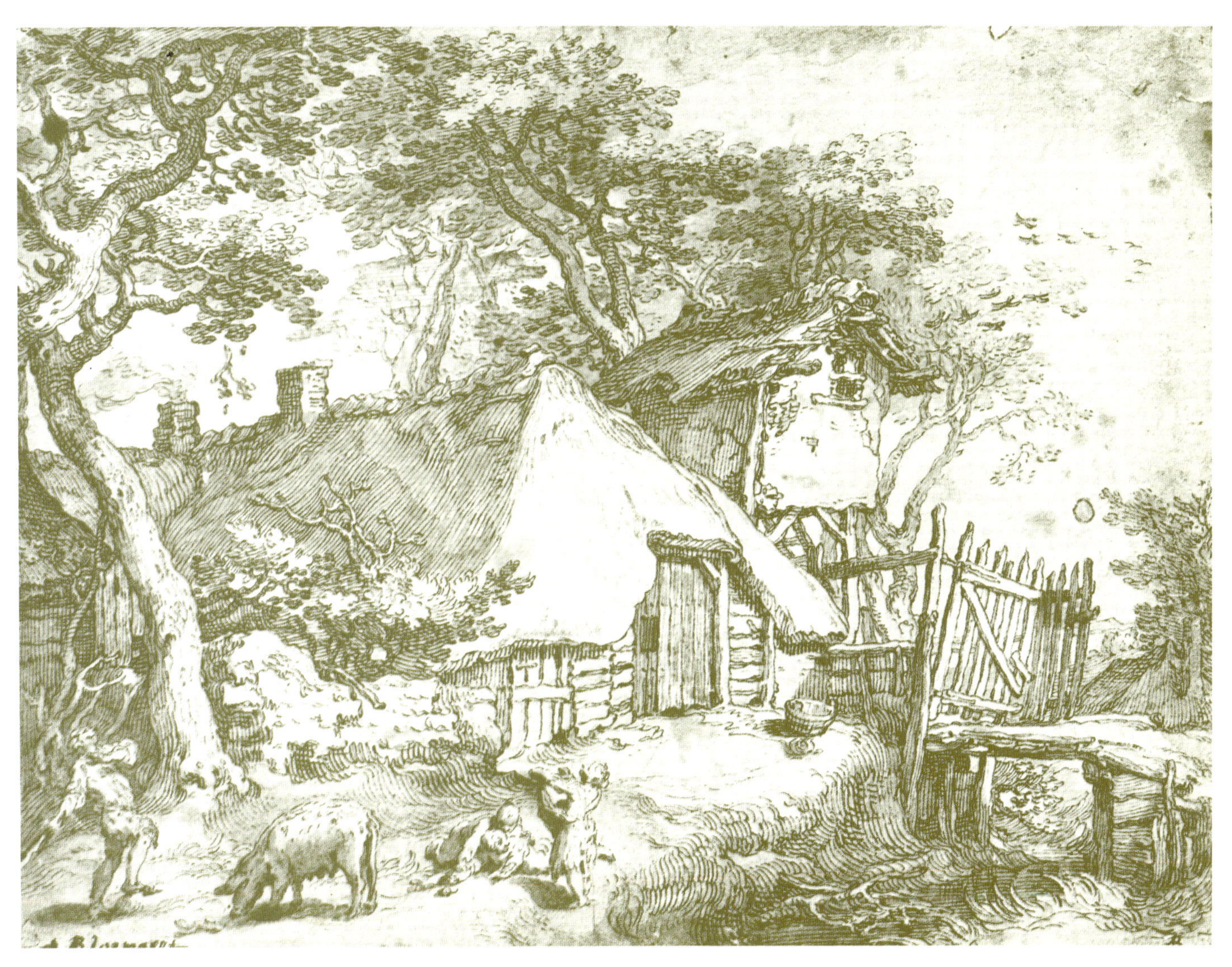

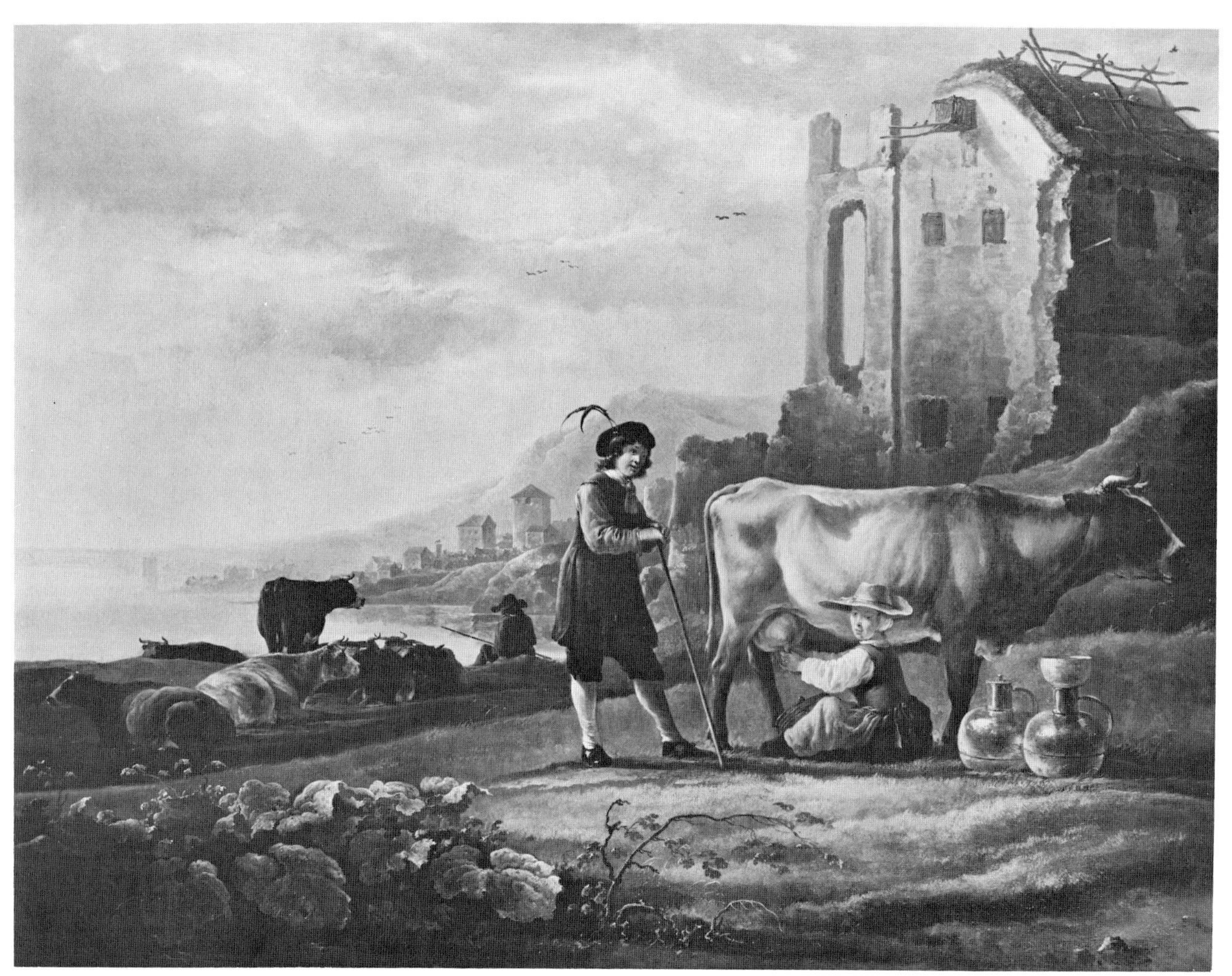

Landscape With Cattle, by Aelbert Cuyp, (1620-1691); The Detroit Institute of Arts.

Holland in the 17th century was proud of its prosperity and its recently-won freedom from Spanish domination. Dutch artists enjoyed painting the beauty of their native country. As people in the growing towns prospered, they were able to buy paintings for their homes. They often commissioned artists to paint their portraits, their possessions and their family activities.

Aelbert Cuyp (Coip) lived in Dordecht, where his work was popular among his farmer neighbors. He was a master of landscapes and animals, and a good portrait painter, too. So, he could please his clients with "portraits" of their cattle or of themselves!

In *Landscape with Cattle* people, cattle, and countryside are all combined to form a pleasant picture of country life. The two young people are carefully dressed and posed for an informal portrait. Cuyp emphasizes a feeling of calm and contentment. The cows, resting after grazing, are watched over by a cowherd. Their long, low curving shapes are repeated in the clump of leaves and the plant in the foreground. Even the young man's feathered cap repeats the same gentle line. Flecks of paint capture the flickering light on the leaves and on the jugs of milk. The play of light and shadow on the cow being milked is the result of careful study. Notice the hazy light and the cloud-filled sky. Cuyp's skill in painting effects of light and atmosphere has been admired by many later artists.

Thousands of years separate the picture on the opposite page of the bull in a barn from this one of a huge, wild bull charging across the wall of a cave in France. The domesticated bull is powerful, but it has been tamed.

The artist's task varies in different times and different cultures. The cave painting of the *Black Bull* may have been part of a magic or religious rite that would ensure success to the hunters. Many similar paintings in prehistoric caves show the hunted animal being struck by spears. Scholars think such a scene was painted in hope that it might become fact. In a sense the artist was a kind of magician. He had a purpose beyond showing what a bull looked like. Yet he must have studied the movement and appearance of live bulls carefully in order to draw them so well.

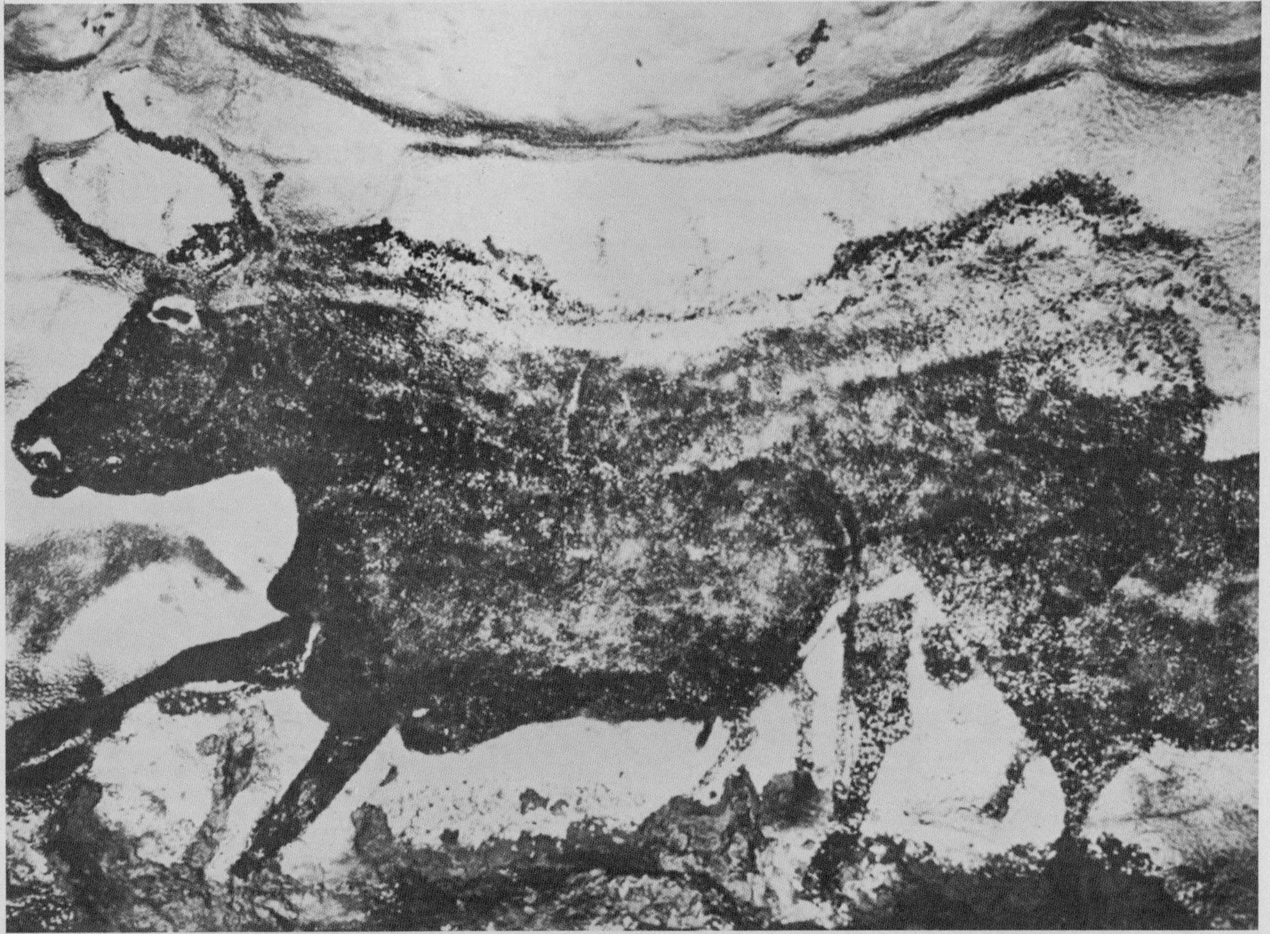

Black Bull, Paleolithic, (about 25,000 BC); Lascaux Caves, Dordogne, French Embassy Press and Information Division.

Honoré Fragonard (on-aw-ray frah-go-nar) drew with a fine brush, using both thin, delicate flecks and lines, and long sweeping strokes. His study of a bull is one of several he made as preparatory sketches for a landscape painting. It was much easier for Fragonard to sit in a barn to make his careful drawing than it must have been for the pre-historic cave painter to watch his wild bull and then to paint it from memory.

Fragonard was a popular artist whose works were commissioned by wealthy Frenchmen. He usually painted portraits of elegant ladies and gentlemen, or historical and mythological subjects. In the latter part of the 18th century a longing for simple farm life had become popular among some of the city people. Fragonard found them an appreciative audience for the country scenes he enjoyed painting.

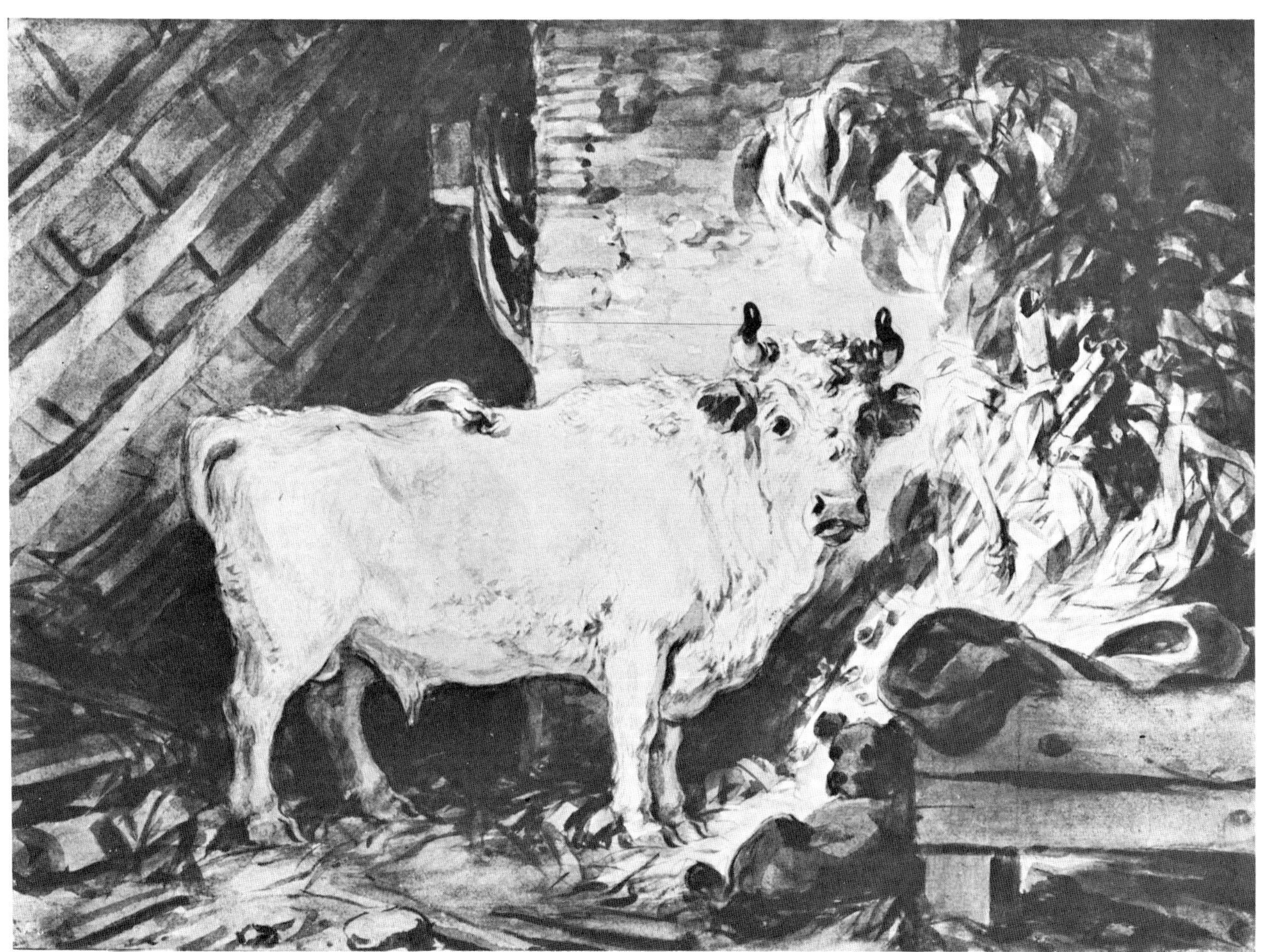

Bull, by Honoré Fragonard, (1732-1806); Albertina, Vienna.

Jean Francois Millet (zhan fran-swah millay) grew up on a French farm and knew the hard work of a farmer from personal experience. However, as a boy he showed talent at drawing, and he was encouraged by his parents to become an artist. For a time he studied and painted in Paris, but finally he moved to the small village of Barbizon where he might live more simply.

Friends who visited him and his family at Barbizon found him working in his garden each morning, dressed in ordinary farmer's clothes. The rest of the day he would paint in his studio. Sometimes a farmer or his wife would pose for Millet, but most of his paintings were based on drawings done while watching the neighboring farmers work.

The Buckwheat Harvest shows a group of farm workers busy threshing. The frenzy of activity, with flails swinging above the men's heads and dust flying, is contrasted with the slower movements of the women in the foreground. Millet admired and respected the honesty, hard work and simplicity of his subjects. His admiration seems to show in the way he painted them.

The Buckwheat Harvest, by Jean Francois Millet, (1814-1875); Courtesy, Museum of Fine Arts, Boston.

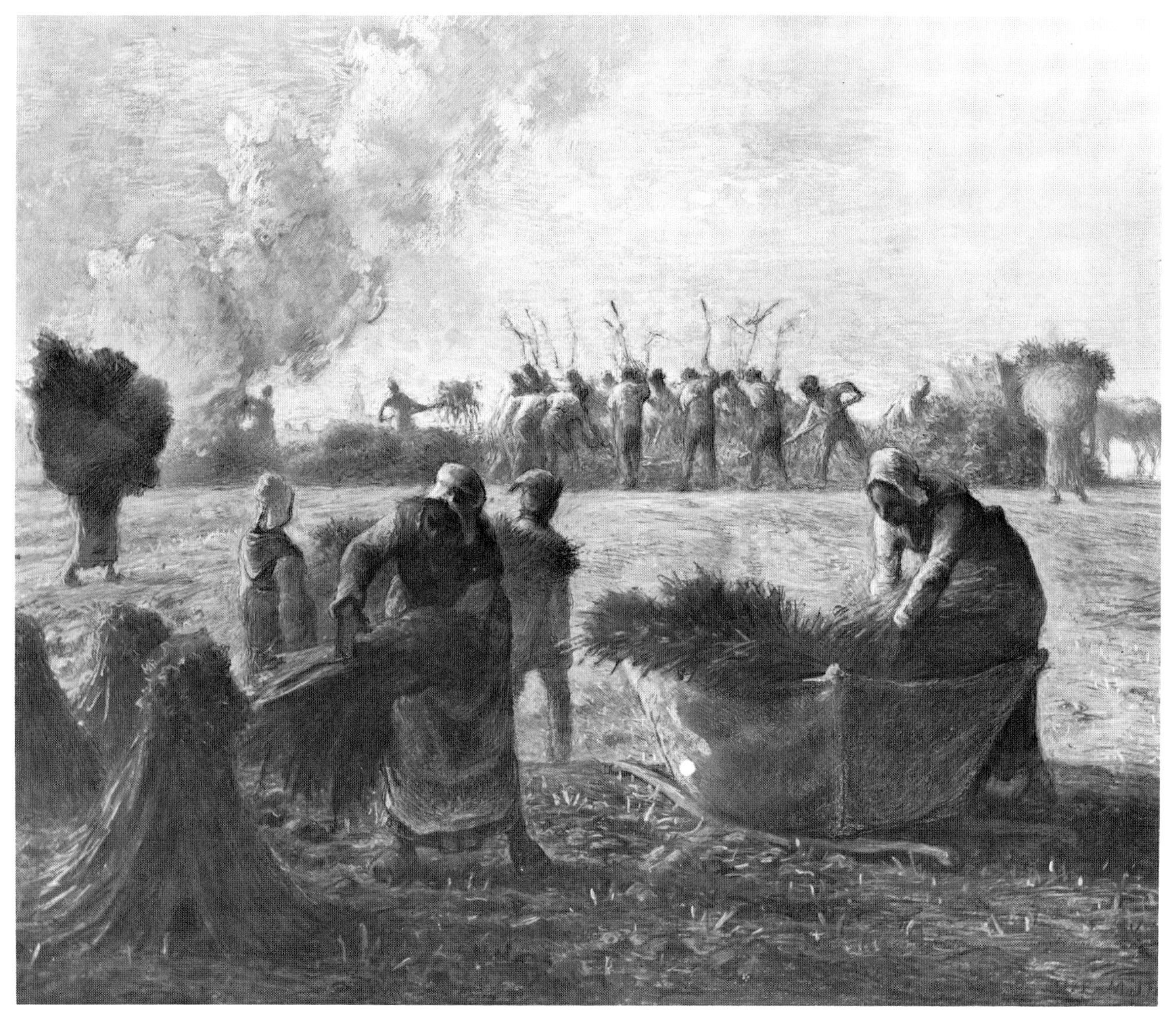

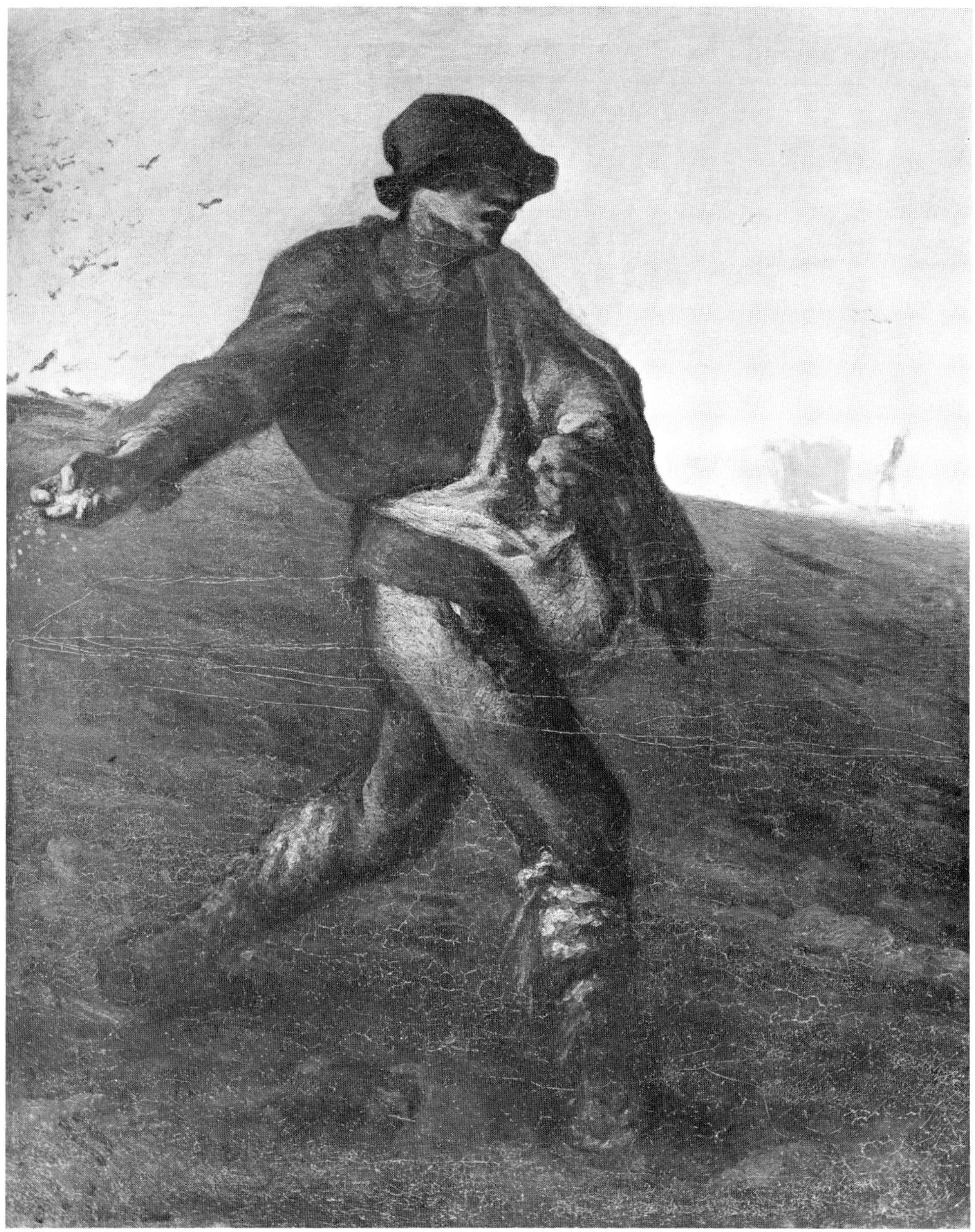

The Sower is a painting that sums up Millet's feeling about the farmer. He is a solid figure, a giant of the earth, walking alone across the fields. He tosses seed into the air with a long swinging motion as he walks. This marks the beginning of the long growing season, and many months of labor lie ahead before there is flour for bread.

People were somewhat surprised, at first, by Millet giving this much importance to the farmer, painting him as if he were a hero. But most came to understand the message of Millet's painting. For where would man be without food to eat?

The Sower, (about 1850); by Jean Francois Millet, Courtesy, Museum of Fine Arts, Boston.

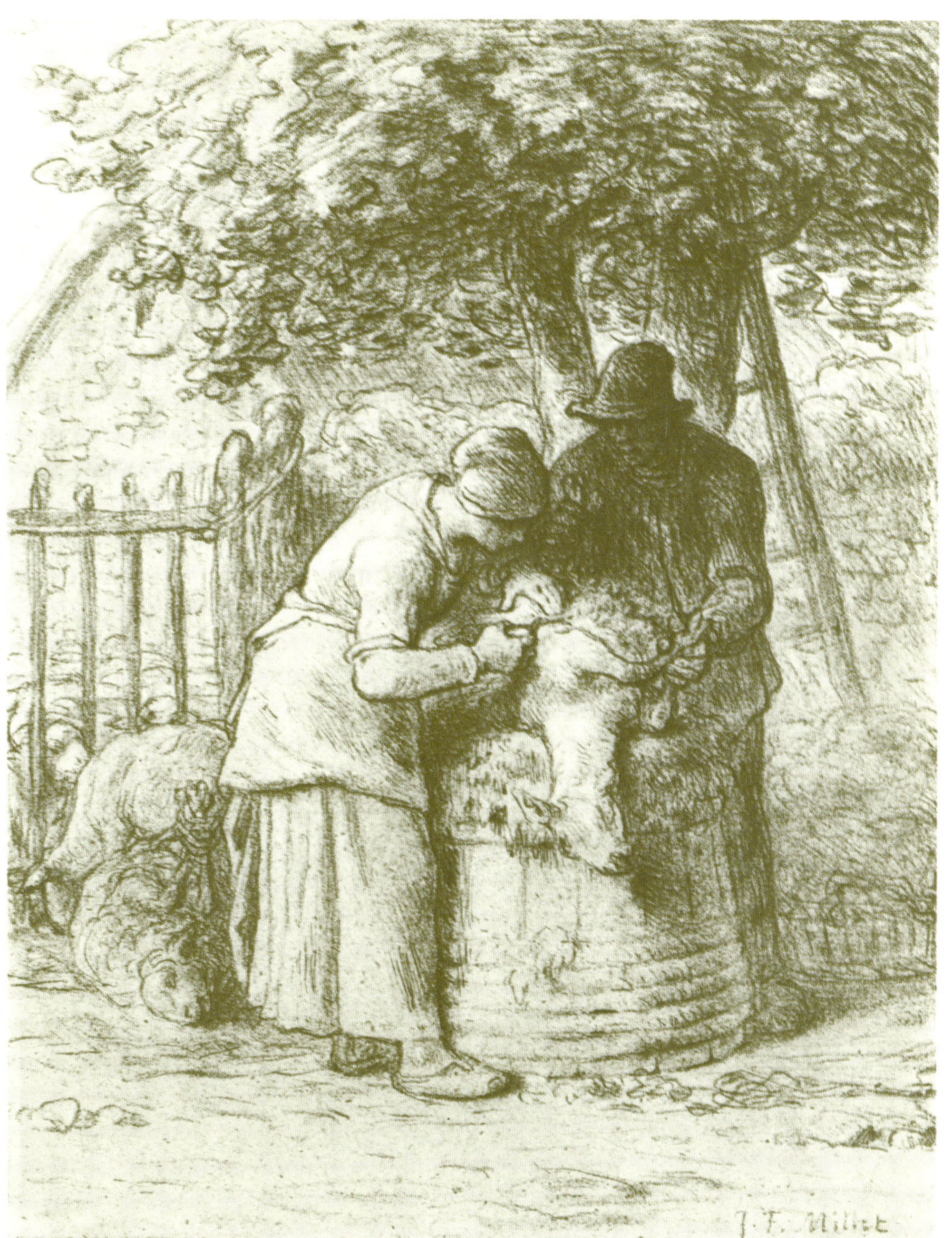

Millet's charcoal drawing *Sheep Shearing* shows the entire composition that he would use for a future finished painting. He has planned not only the figures, but also the placement of the dark and light areas of the painting. This drawing was made in black and white, but the final picture is painted in greens, warm earthy yellows and brownish tones, the colors he often used.

Here Millet records the task of shearing. The farmer holds a sheep firmly while his wife cuts the fleece. She will later card and spin the wool, weave and sew the cloth. Clothes for a 19th century French farm family usually came from the family's own sheep.

Sheep Shearing, (about 1861); by Jean Francois Millet, The Metropolitan Museum of Art, Gift of G. Louise Robinson, 1940.

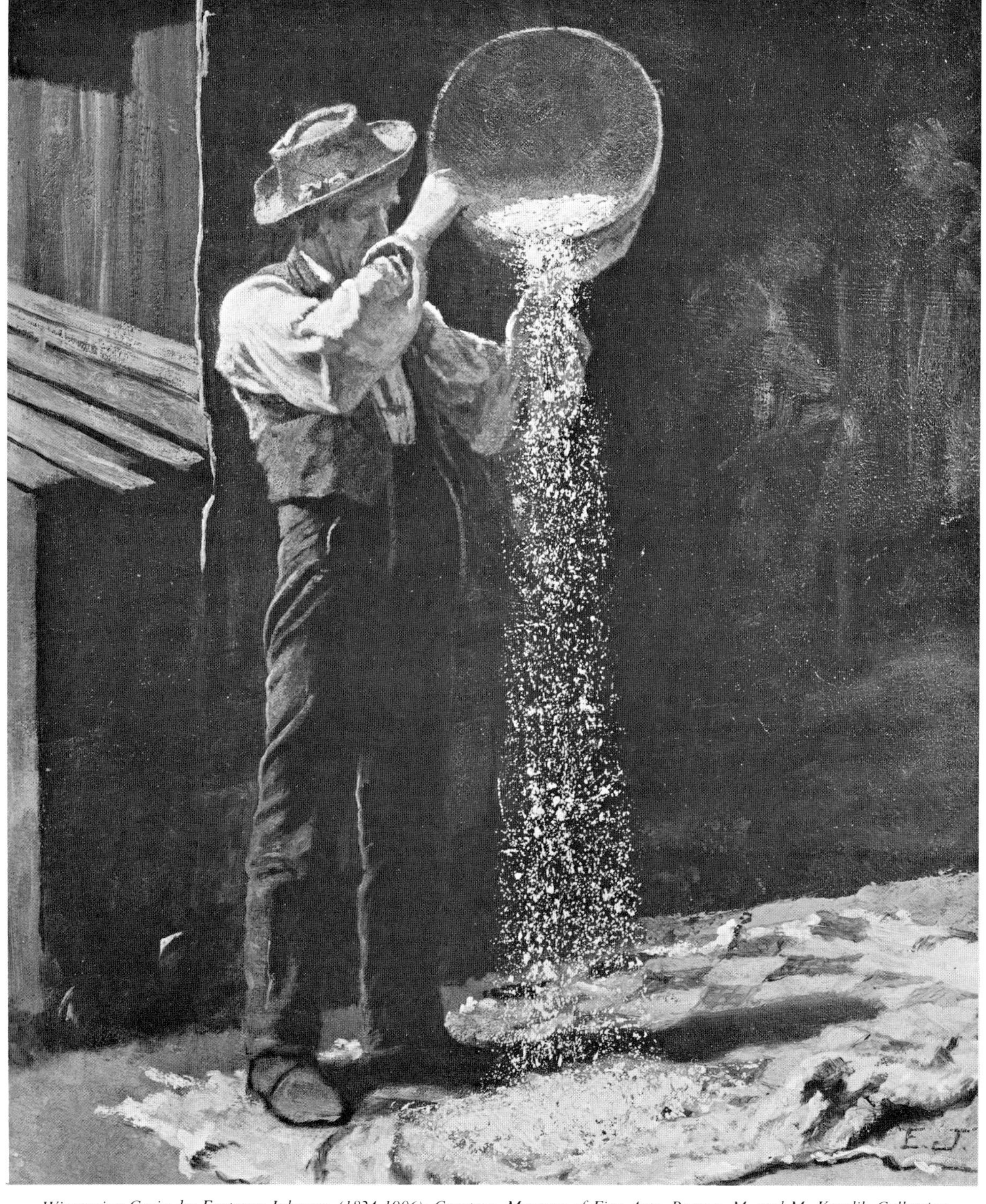

Winnowing Grain, by Eastman Johnson, (1824-1906); Courtesy, Museum of Fine Arts, Boston, M. and M. Karolik Collection.

Eastman Johnson shows a man winnowing grain. He pours the grain from the basket to separate the wheat from the chaff. The lightweight husks blow away, and the seed falls to the ground. Before the use of modern machinery, the harvesting of grain and preparing it for grinding into flour was a tedious job. Each step of the process required a great deal of time. Late in the century, mechanical reapers and other farm machinery speeded up the process. But here, Johnson shows an activity that hadn't changed greatly in many centuries. Do you remember the Egyptian *Harvest Scene?*

Like Millet, Johnson was a realist. He had no illusion that farm life was easy. The farmer is a plain, straightforward laborer. A job is to be done, and he does it. Eastman Johnson found beauty in this ordinary subject. Perhaps he was attracted by the grain poured through the air and the contrast of gold against warm brownish shadows. Perhaps he found the man's pose an interesting one to draw. It may have been a combination of both reasons. Johnson used a strong side light to pick out the solid form of the figure and the folds of his clothing. The shimmer of the grain is highlighted against the dark interior of the barn. A few brushstrokes indicate the shadowy figures of two people at work in the background.

Winslow Homer was an American artist who learned to draw early in life. He had some training but was largely self-taught. As an illustrator for a weekly magazine he drew scenes of the Civil War to accompany news stories. He also drew subjects from New York city life. But he disliked large cities. When he gave up his career as an illustrator to become a painter, he found some of his favorite subjects in the country. He loved fishing and hunting and spent a great deal of time throughout his life in rural areas or at the seashore.

About the middle of the 19th century, many artists began to represent the life of ordinary people in casual, everyday situations. Homer's work showed people at work or at play, in the country, on farms, in fishing villages, at seaside resorts, or hunting and fishing in the wilderness. Most of his farm subjects were painted in the 1870's and 1880's.

In *The Dinner Horn,* painted in oil, the farmwife is shown as she calls the men home from the fields to eat. She blows a horn instead of ringing a dinner bell. Her figure is modelled in simple areas of light and shadow as she stands in the shade of the porch, a solid figure placed right in the middle of the canvas. The brilliant light of a warm summer day can be seen through the door and reflected in the vine leaves on the trellis. The farmwife's pose may be quiet, but her bent arms carry your eye to each side of the painting. They also form part of long diagonal direction lines that reach from corner to corner. The center of her back is the point at which the diagonal lines cross. This *composition,* or arrangement, makes her stand out as the center of interest.

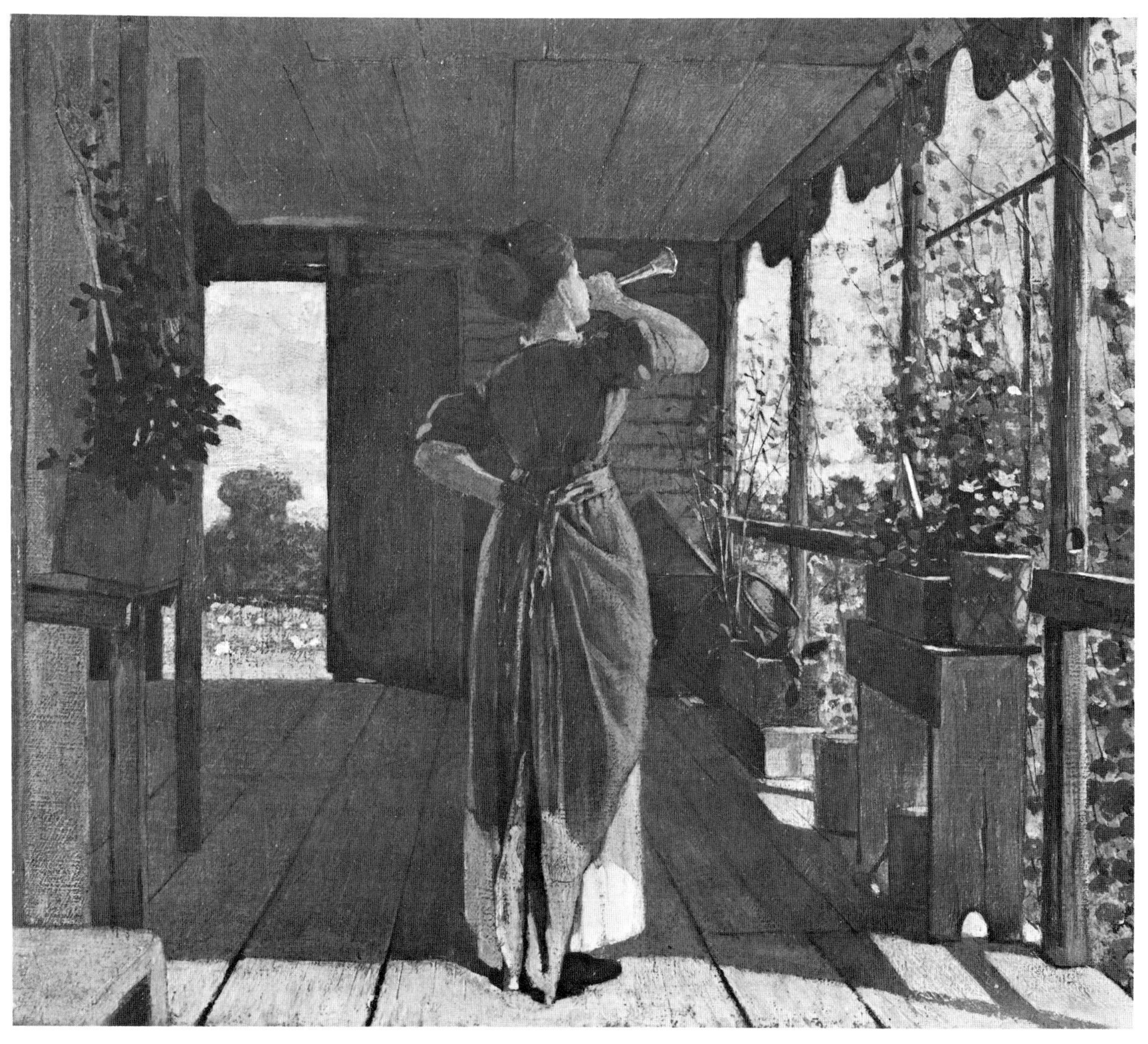

The Dinner Horn, by Winslow Homer, (1836-1910); The Detroit Institute of Arts.

Farm Woman Going Home, by Vincent van Gogh, (1853-1890); Kroller-Muller Museum, Otterlo.

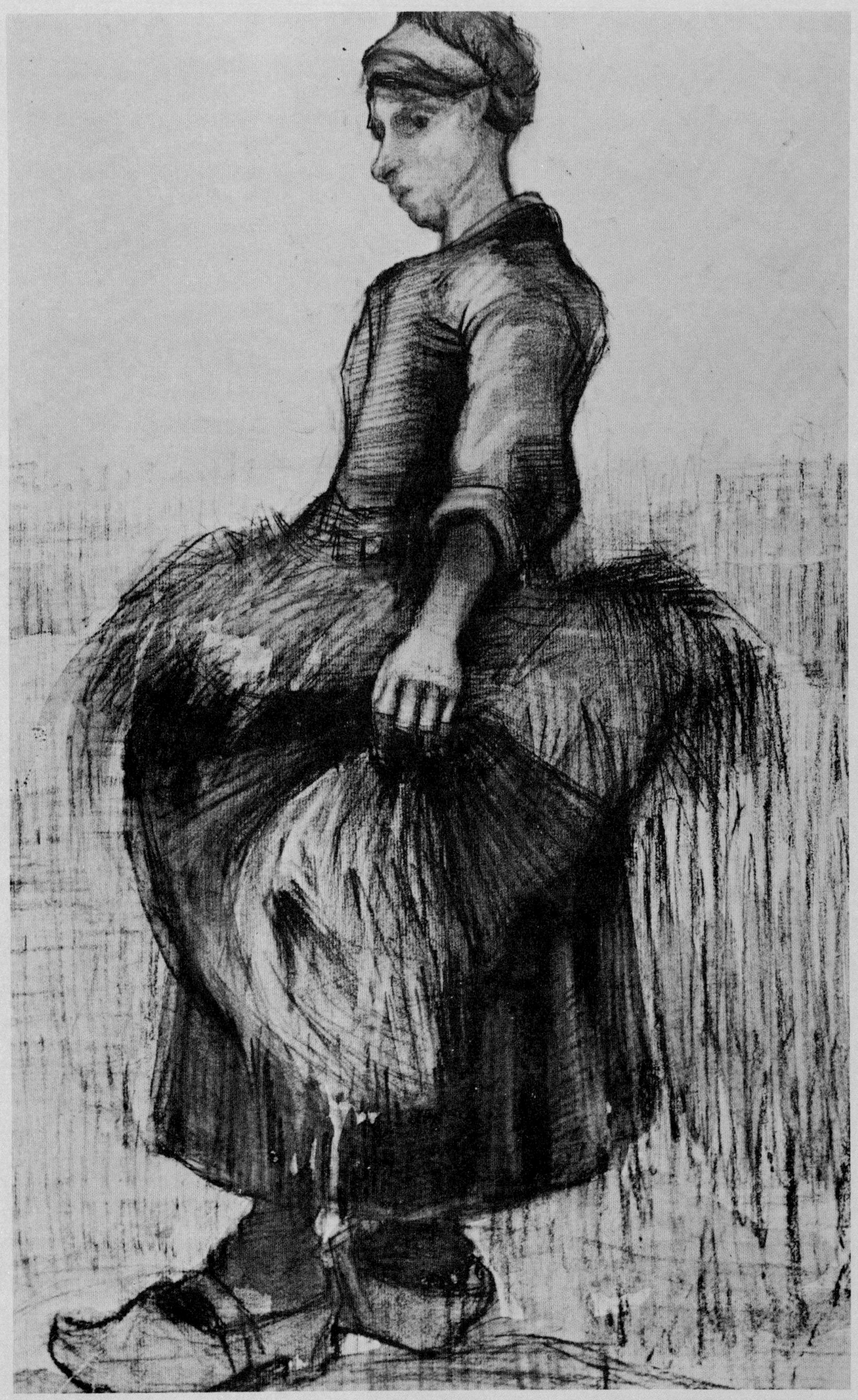

The Gleaner, by Jean Francois Millet, The Albertina, Vienna.

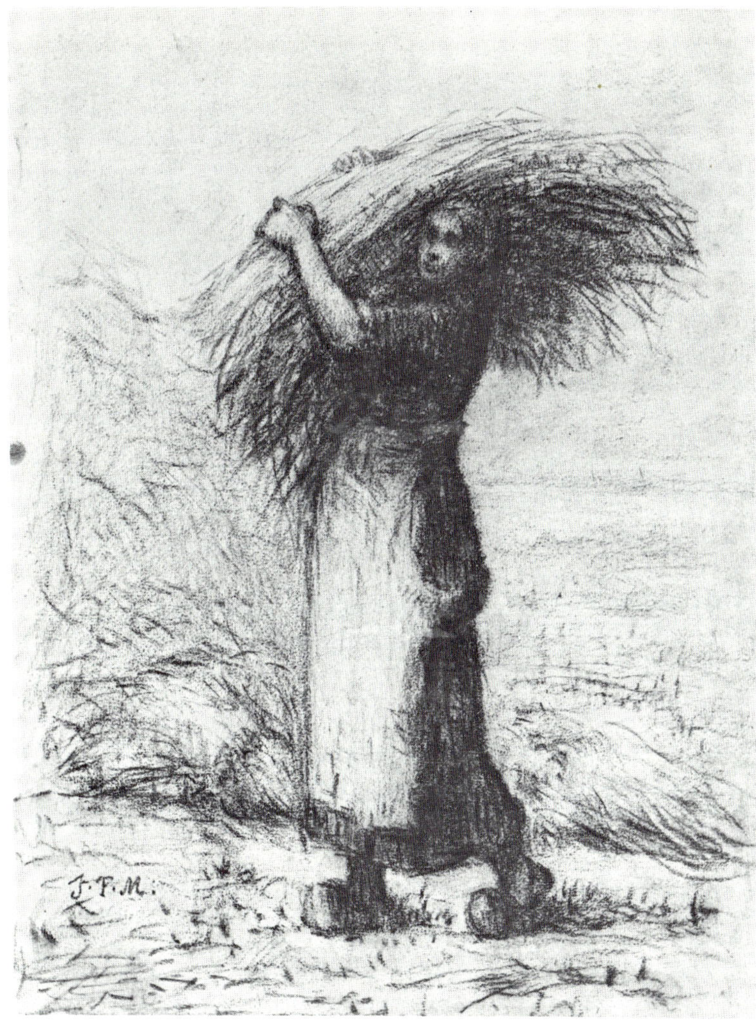

Vincent Van Gogh (van goh) drew a Dutch farm woman carrying a bundle of grain in her apron. The woman is not beautiful, but her sturdiness is impressive. Like Jean Francois Millet, who made the drawing of *The Gleaner,* Van Gogh believed in the dignity of work and the importance of the farmer. Van Gogh also admired Millet's paintings of farm subjects and sometimes painted his own versions of them. In this case, however, he and Millet simply made drawings of a similar subject that might be seen almost anywhere during harvest time. Van Gogh's woman seems solid and rock-like, with her wooden shoes firmly planted on the ground. She seems to have paused to allow the artist to sketch her. Each line of the drawing is as firm and strong as she is.

Millet's woman moves slowly as she carries her awkward, heavy load. The short, flickering strokes follow the long sweeping curve formed by her body and the grain she has gathered. There is a kind of hazy feeling to this drawing that makes it seem gentle and soft in comparison to Van Gogh's.

It is easy to see that artists differ in their way of drawing, just as people differ in their handwriting. You wouldn't easily mistake a drawing by Vincent Van Gogh for one by Millet after looking at these two examples, would you?

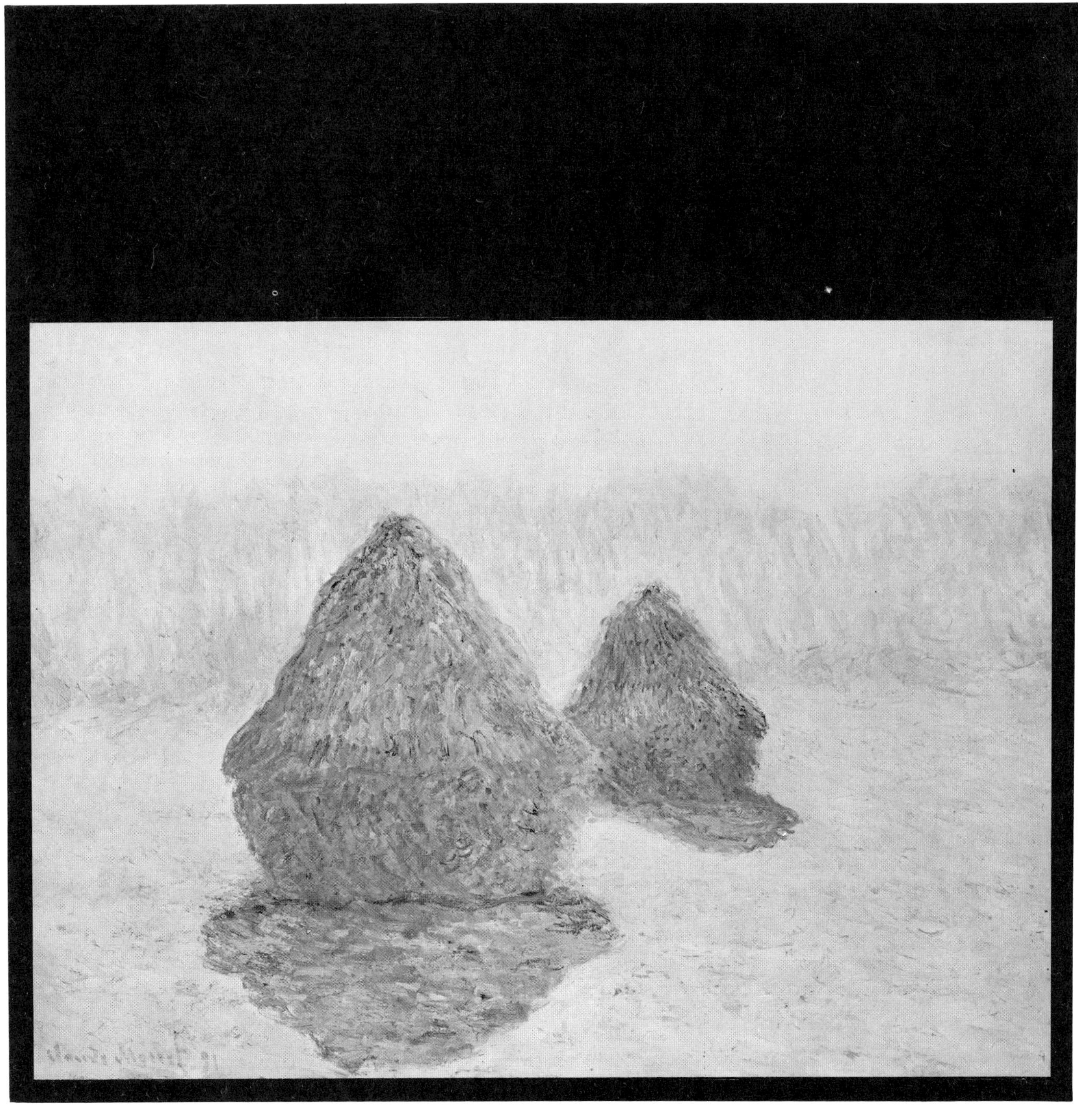

Haystacks In Snow, by Claude Monet, (1840-1926). The Metropolitan Museum of Art, New York, Bequest of Mrs. H. O. Havemeyer, 1929. The H. O. Havemeyer Collection.

During the late 19th century a group of French artists developed a new way of painting the effects of color and light as they saw them in nature. They used pure colors placed on the canvas with short brushstrokes. The colors they used were those closest to the colors of the rainbow. When a picture painted in the new way was seen from a distance the colors would seem to blend, or be mixed together, by the eye. The painters felt that this produced effects similar to the brilliance of colors seen out-of-doors in daylight. They felt that the traditional way of painting by mixing colors on a palette and using many greyed and brownish tones was suited to painting in a studio. But they wanted to paint the beauty of their gardens, the countryside, and the color and variety of Paris streets. This meant that they painted outdoors instead of making sketches and then painting the final landscape indoors as had usually been done.

Claude Monet (clode mo-nay) probably explored this way of painting more than anyone else. A painting of his called *Impression—Sunrise* (1872), which was exhibited along with the works of Renoir, Degas, Pissarro, and others, gave the new way of painting its name. As often happens with new and unfamiliar styles, the critics and public did not understand the blurred and sketchy paintings. One critic complained that Monet's painting was "just an impression." That was how the entire group of painters came to be called *Impressionists.*

When Monet painted *Haystacks in Snow,* he was not really concerned with the farm or farmers. He needed some simple objects that would not move while he studied the effects of light at different times of day. At first he thought he would need only two canvases—one for sunshine and the other for cloudy light. He very quickly discovered how short a time any single light effect lasted. In the early morning the haystacks seemed pale and clear in color, at midday they were strong and bright, during a colorful sunset they reflected warm reds and pinks, and on a dark day they were misty and grey. So Monet made an entire series of paintings showing haystacks throughout the day and in different seasons. This painting of haystacks is misty and light with shimmering white snow.

Georges Seurat learned the Impressionist way of painting with small strokes of pure color. But he wanted to be still more effective in capturing the true brilliance and whiteness of daylight. He had read scientific writings on color and light, and on these theories he based a system of painting. He worked out careful proportions for the amounts of various colors needed to give the right effect. According to his system, an area of grass would be painted with dabs of green, but with smaller amounts of all of the other colors as well. Grass appears green because it reflects green light waves, but some of the other colors of light are also reflected in small amounts. Seurat would paint shaded areas of grass with strokes of violet, blue, yellow, and green. There would also be a few strokes of red and orange. Sunny areas of grass would be painted with more green and yellow, and less violet and blue. Red and orange would also be increased in order to give a warmer effect to the green. Seurat painted his large pictures in the studio, depending on his system in order to apply the right amounts of color. He painted many smaller canvases out-of-doors, noting color effects that he might use in his final paintings. *The Farm Laborer with a Hoe* is one of these studies painted in oil. Seurat's main interest was in color and light, especially the way in which they showed the solid form of the man's body. All the shapes are simple, and details are omitted. Seurat painted a farmer, but his *real* interest was light.

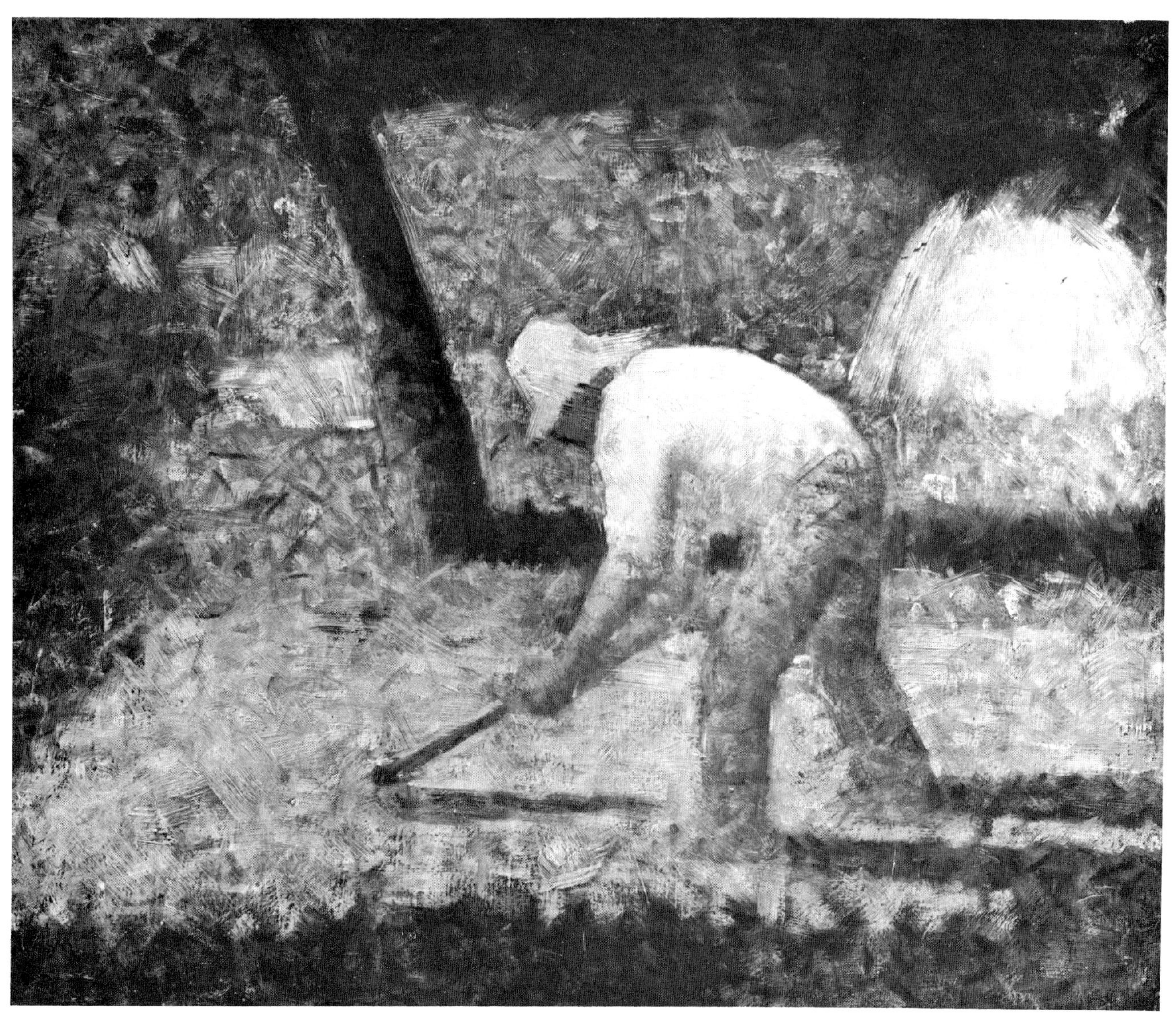

Farm Laborer With Hoe, (1884); by Georges-Pierre Seurat, (1859-1891), The Solomon R. Guggenheim Museum, New York.

Pieter Brueghel showed how many farm laborers were needed to do the harvesting in the 16th century. But in the 20th century machines take the place of human labor. Even larger and more efficient machines have come into use since Ogden Pleissner painted this scene in the 1930's. Still, this harvest scene would have been a marvel to Brueghel's peasants—or even to Millet's farmers in the 19th century.

In the United States during the 1930's and 1940's, many artists painted scenes of American life. They painted farmers, miners, factory and oil field workers, and people in the crowded cities and the small towns. The paintings were not always pretty or happy. Life was changing rapidly, and the artists wanted to record everything they saw.

In this oil painting *The Reapers,* Pleissner showed midwestern farming with its endless fields of grain. The two farmers are silhouetted against a grey-blue clouded sky. One drives the tractor and the other controls the reaper as it cuts, gathers, ties, and drops the wheat on the ground, ready to be picked up. Two men can harvest a great deal of wheat quickly, but to what distances their fields stretch! Their day's work is no easier than that of the 16th century peasants, but how much more they accomplish.

The Reapers, by Ogden Pleissner, (1905-); The Minneapolis Institute of Arts.

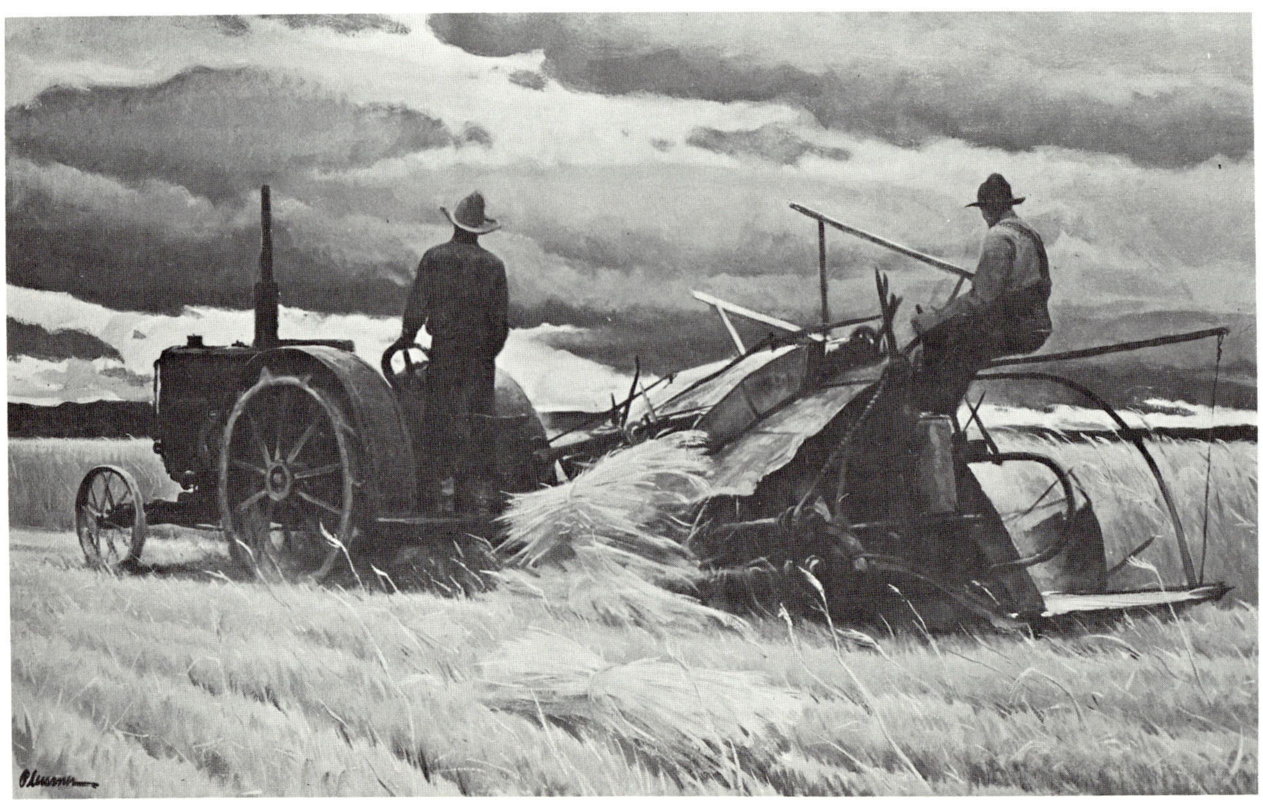

During the 1920's Mexican artists became very conscious of their heritage. Like artists in other countries that had won independence, the Mexican painters turned to subjects from their own history. Public buildings were decorated with *murals,* or wall paintings showing life in the days before the Spanish Conquest, as well as many aspects of the modern life of the Mexican. Painters also became interested in native Mexican art. Diego Rivera (di-AY-go ri-VAIR-uh) admired the large, simple shapes of Pre-Conquest Indian art. He began to use similar shapes on his own paintings.

Sugar Cane is a *fresco,* or a painting on wet plaster. It shows Indians at work on a sugar cane plantation. They are cutting the sugar cane and carrying it in heavy bundles to the mill to be processed. The Indians were hired hands on the plantation. Rivera shows the overseer on horseback. (Do you remember the overseer leaning on his staff in the Egyptian *Harvest Scene?)* The manager or owner of the plantation is lying in a hammock on the porch. Rivera was critical of the way in which the Indians had been forced to work for the landowner instead of having more land and independence to farm for themselves. They were allowed only small patches of land on which to grow food for their families.

In the foreground, Indian children gather coconuts. Perhaps they intend to bring them to the workers for a refreshing drink of coconut milk.

Sugar Cane, (1930); by Diego Rivera, (1886-1957), Philadelphia Museum of Art.

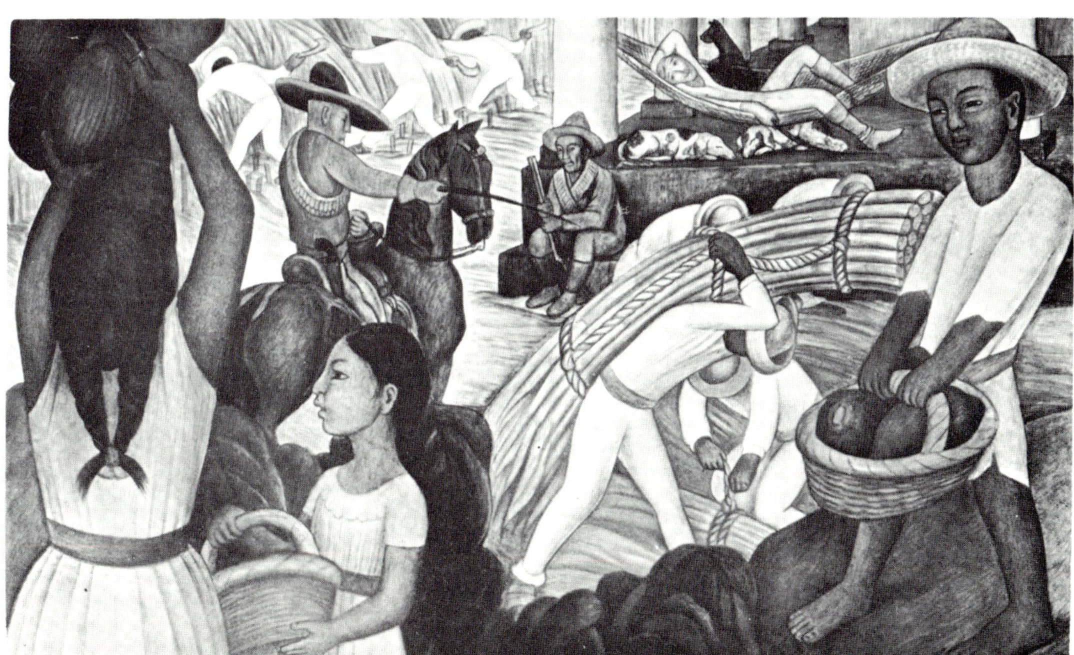

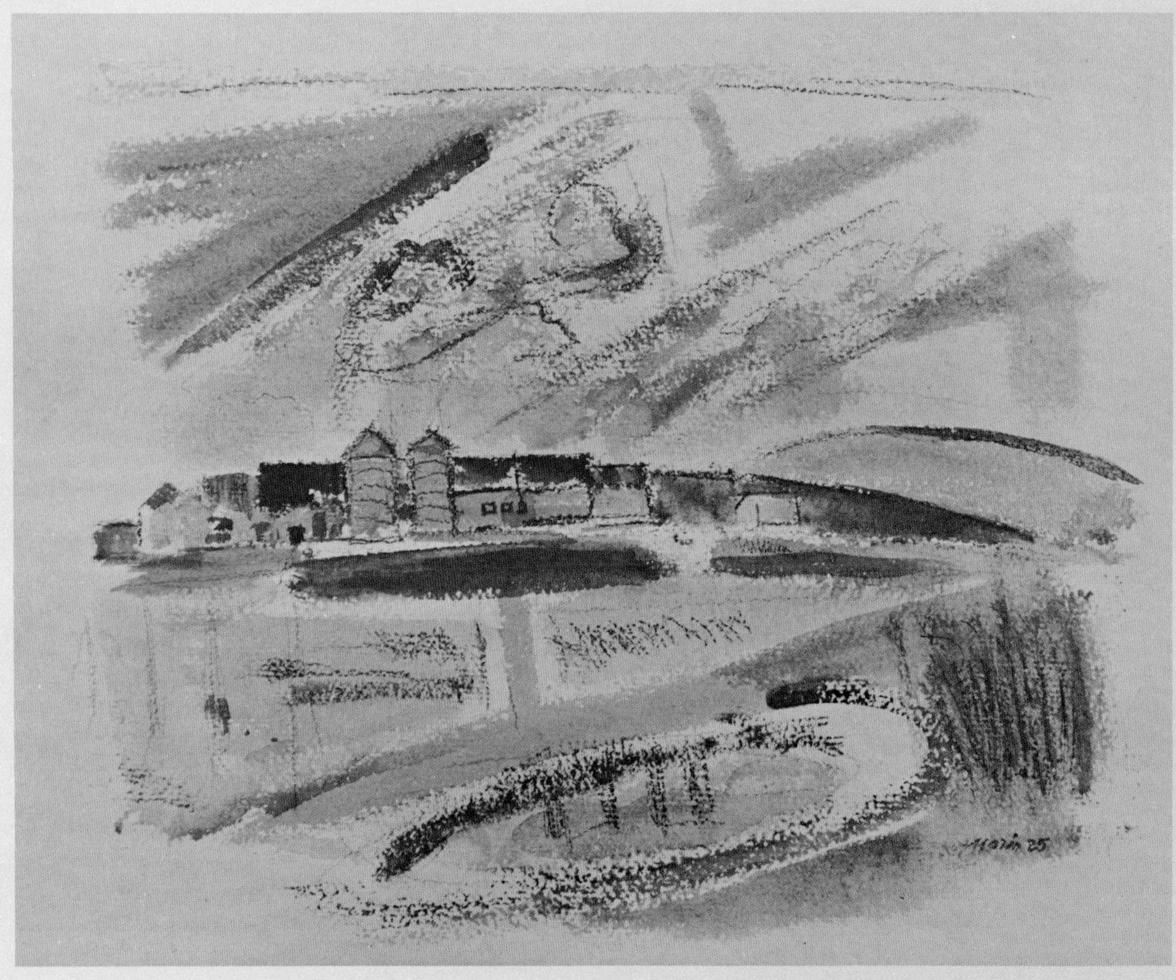

Barn In the Berkshires, by John Marin, (1870-1953); Courtesy, The Brooklyn Museum, New York.

Large, bold brushstrokes sweep across the sky in *Barn in the Berkshires.* A long curve marks a hill. Two strokes encircle a pond. Every line and shape is appropriate to the open countryside. No little strokes or details slow down the sense of movement that John Marin (MAIR-in) achieved in this watercolor. Only in the main subject of silos and barn does he use detail.

Marin's style of painting is a bit like shorthand. Taken out of their place in the painting, some patches of color might not be identified. But seen together they are easily understood. The zigzag in the sky exaggerates the piling up of clouds into mountain-like forms. A few lines brushed up and down represent wheat or tall grass. The simplified shapes, lines and angles of Marin's paintings are similar to those of the *Cubist* abstract painters, who painted objects in terms of their basic structure. But Marin used the forms in a way that was entirely his own, in order to show space and rhythmic movement.

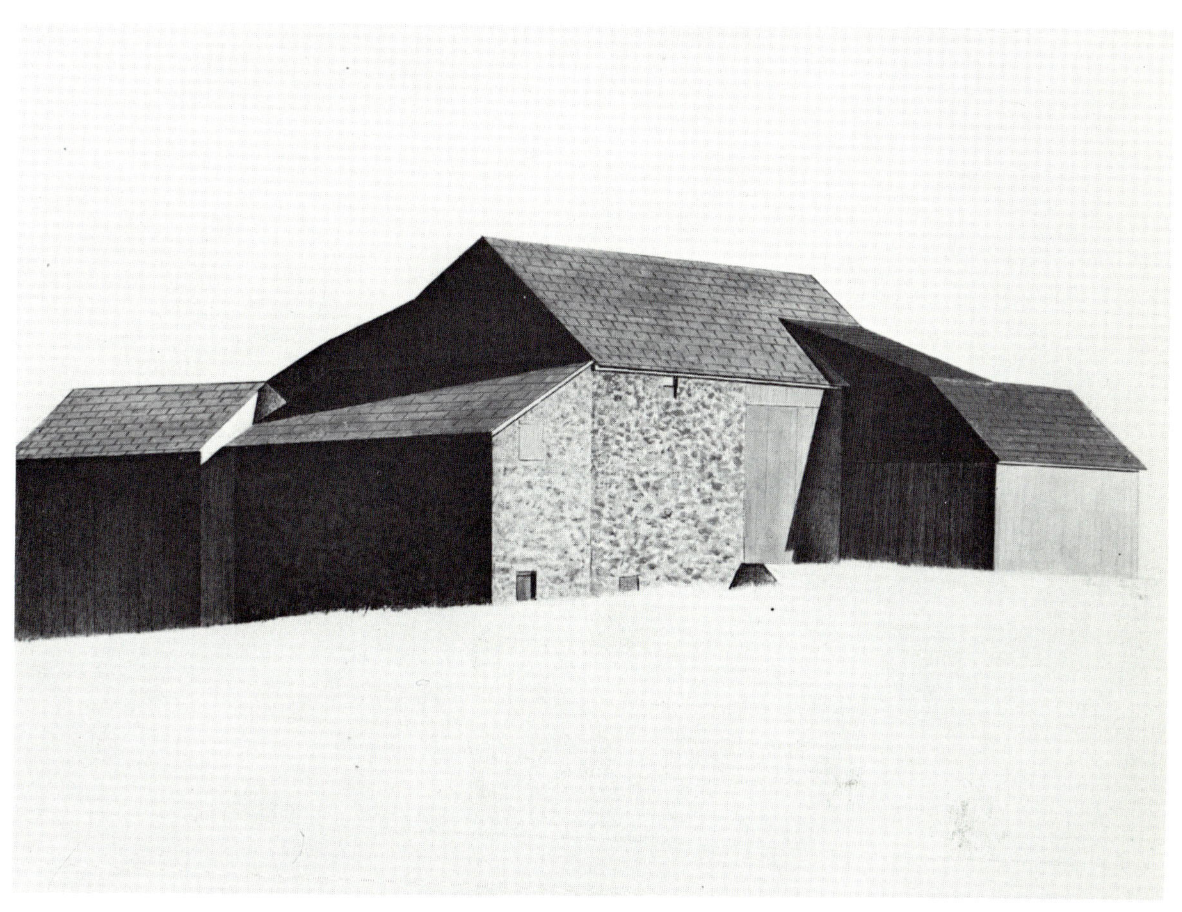

Bucks County Barn, (1923); by Charles Sheeler, (1883-1965); Collection of Whitney Museum of American Art, N.Y.

It may not surprise you to learn that Charles Sheeler worked for a time as a professional photographer. In *Bucks County Barn* both the careful drawing and the emphasis on light and shade suggest a record made by a camera. This picture is totally different in feeling from John Marin's painting. Sheeler's work, in crayon and tempera, seems to reproduce every stone and board. He is fascinated by the shapes and shadows of the barn. They help to define the solidness of the building.

Although at first the picture may seem like a photograph, it is actually quite different. The camera records everything, but the painter decides how much should be included. Sheeler left out the background, thereby emphasizing the odd shape of the building. The white background of the sky and ground areas suggests the blinding glare of strong sunlight.

Like John Marin and Winslow Homer, Sheeler painted subjects that are familiar scenes in the United States. He found beautiful forms not only in barns, but also in factories, cities, ships, locomotives, and room interiors. He rarely included people in his paintings. For Sheeler, things seem to stand for the people who use them.

Thanksgiving, (1935); by Doris Lee, (1905-), The Art Institute of Chicago, Mr. and Mrs. Frank G. Logan purchase prize.

Doris Lee seems to have been chuckling as she painted the preparations for Thanksgiving Day dinner in a farm kitchen. Everything is happening at once. There is a great deal of bustling and hurrying about. The turkey is being basted, pie dough is being rolled thin, and the table is being set. It seems that the artist remembered her own family holidays and wanted to recapture every detail. Like many other painters at this time Doris Lee was recording an aspect of American life.

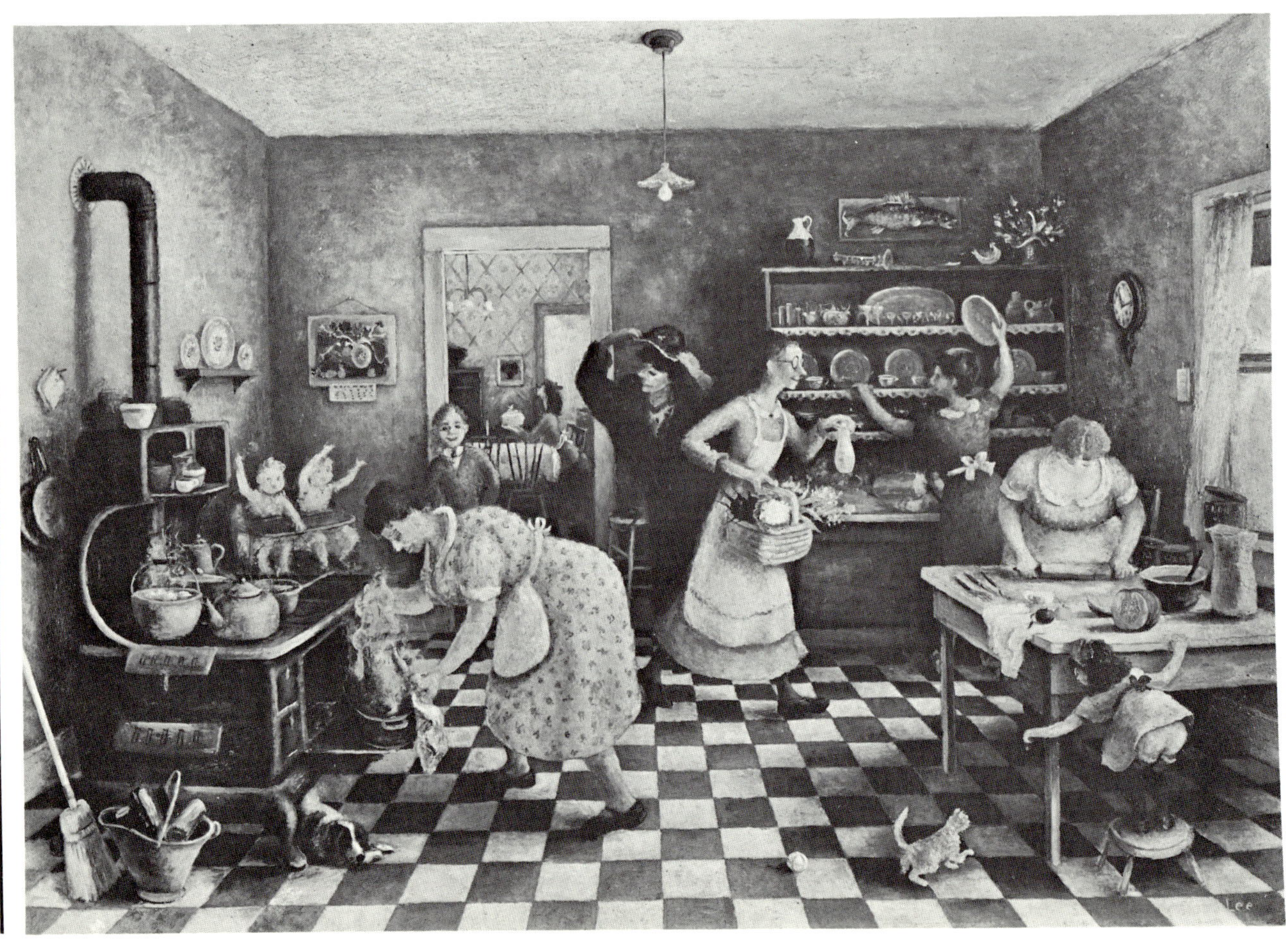

I and the Village, (1911); by Marc Chagall, (1889-). Collection, The Museum of Modern Art, New York, Mrs. Simon Guggenheim Fund.

Marc Chagall (shah-GAHL) grew up in the village of Vitebsk in Russia. Later, as a young man living in Paris, he painted many scenes of his home, the people and events that he remembered from his childhood.

In dreams, events take place in an unreal order and often seem topsy-turvy. At times in remembering the past, some things stand out more than others, like in a dream, and memory quickly jumps from one idea to another. In *I and the Village,* Chagall combined fragments of many memories of country and village life. A woman milks a cow, a man carries a scythe, a woman looks out of one of a row of wooden houses, and Chagall seems to be having a conversation with another cow. He did not paint the day-to-day reality, but rather those things that delighted him.

Farms and farmers have been shown in works of art in many ways. But they have not often been painted as a kind of joyous, colorful dream or fairytale.

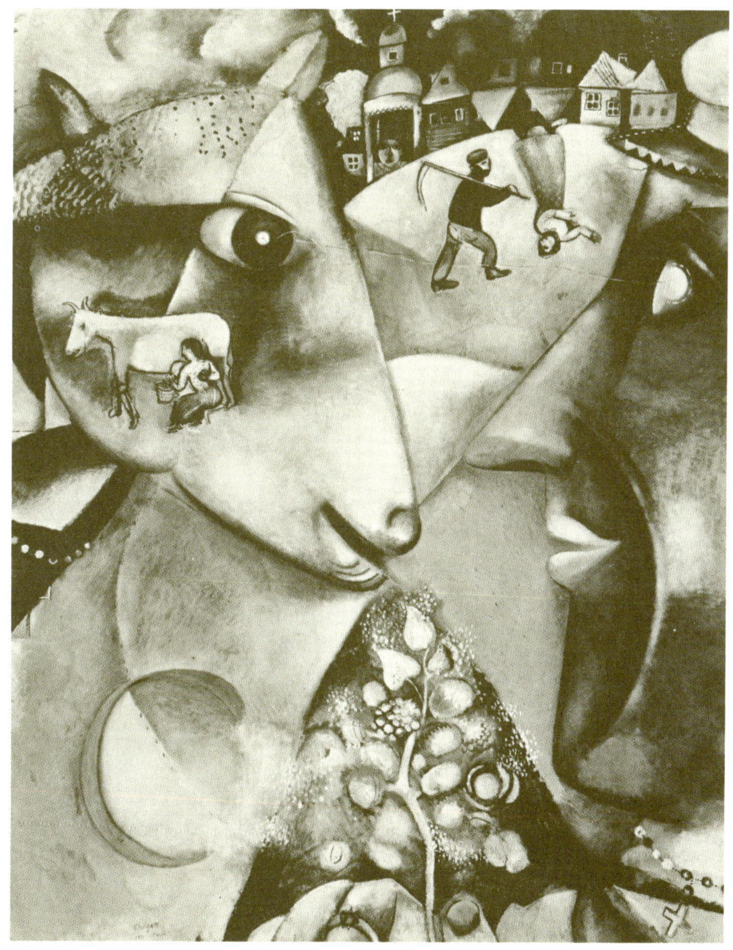

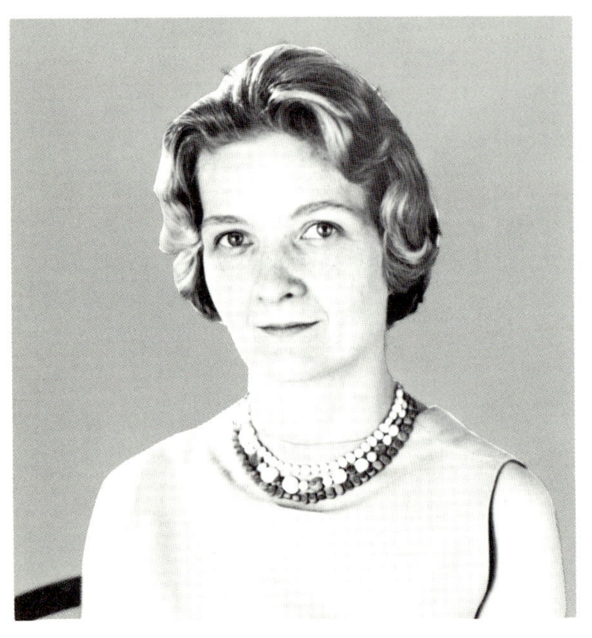

ABOUT THE AUTHOR

Helen B. Harkonen formerly was an Associate Curator at the Walker Art Center. She also was Head of Education at The Minneapolis Institute of Arts and has taught at the University of Minnesota. She has studied both the studio arts and art history. Her B.A. is from the College of the University of Chicago and her B.F.A. and M.F.A. are from the School of the Art Institute of Chicago. At present she is preparing for her doctorate in Art History.

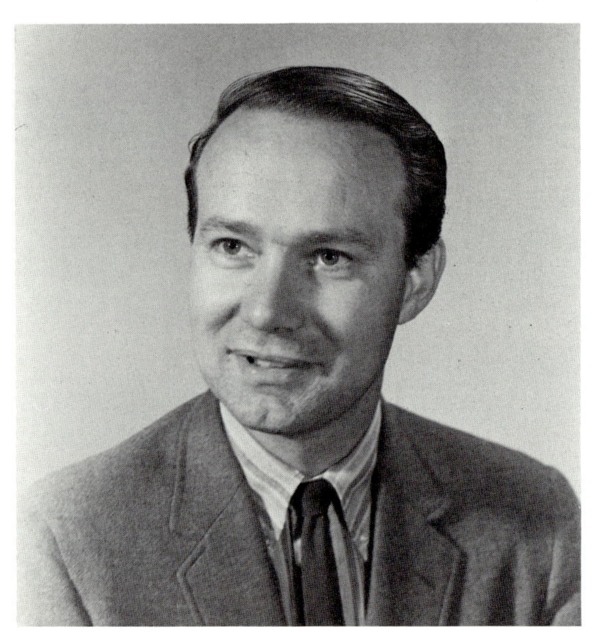

ABOUT THE DESIGNER

Robert Clark Nelson is a distinguished designer with extensive achievements to his credit. He is a graduate of the Minneapolis School of Arts and Bethel College, and is currently an instructor in art, painting and graphic design at the latter institution.

Mr. Nelson's work has been included in five editions of the *Graphic Annual,* and two editions of the *New York Art Directors Annual.* His most recent honor has been the inclusion of four of his posters in the *International Poster Annual,* a Swiss publication covering the poster art of 26 countries.